American Flyer ®

American Flyer ®

CLASSIC TOY TRAINS

Gerry & Janet Souter

FRIEDMAN/FAIRFAX

A FRIEDMAN/FAIRFAX BOOK
© 2002 by Michael Friedman Publishing Group, Inc.

Please visit our website: www.metrobooks.com

American Flyer is the registered trademark of the Lionel Toy Corporation.

Library of Congress Cataloging-in-Publication Data

Souter, Gerry.
    American Flyer : classic toy trains / Gerry and Janet Souter.
        p. cm.
    Includes bibliographical references and index.
    ISBN 1-58663-574-3 (alk. paper)
    1. Railroads—Models. I. Souter, Janet, 1940- II. Title.

TF197 .S6255 2002
625.1'9—dc21

2002023771

Editor: Rosy Ngo
Art Director: Kevin Ullrich
Designer: Kevin Baier
Photography Director: Christopher C. Bain
Production Manager: Michael Vagnetti

Photography: ©Bill Milne

Digital repro by Chroma Graphics
Printed in Belgium by Proost NV

10 9 8 7 6 5 4 3 2 1

Distributed by Sterling Publishing Company, Inc.
387 Park Avenue South
New York, NY 10016
Distributed in Canada by Sterling Publishing
Canadian Manda Group
One Atlantic Avenue, Suite 105
Toronto, Ontario, Canada M6K 3E7
Distributed in Australia by
Capricorn Link (Australia) Pty. Ltd.
P.O. Box 704, Windsor, NSW 2756 Australia

AMERICAN FLYER TRAIN COLLECTIONS

The publisher is indebted to many individuals and clubs for access to their American Flyer collections for the photography in this book. We have identified each collector below, indicating the page number and position of each piece from their collection.

David Avedesian: 1, 2, 6 (bottom), 88–89, 91, 106, 107, 110 (both), 114 (top), 118, 123 (middle right), 126, 127 (top left and right), 128 (right top), 130 (both), 130–131, 135, 137, 140 (bottom), 142 (top), 143 (top), 150 (top), 150–151, 152 (bottom), and 153

Bill Bateman: 7 (inset), 9, 10, 12–13, 15, 18 (bottom), 24–25, 39 (top), 40 (left), 64, and 70–71

Barry Berson: 104–105, 108 (both), 109 (top), 116, 117 (both), 121 (right), 123 (top), 128 (bottom), 141 (top), and 148–149

Courtesy of **Louise S. Coleman-Brown:** 16 (top)

Courtesy of **Kirby Coleman Brown:** 54 (both)

Courtesy of **William L. Coleman:** 23 (upper left), 28

Monte Heppe: 27, 29, 34 (top), 47, 65 (top), 66, 68 (top), 76, 82, 103 (right), 124 (bottom left), 127 (bottom), 129 (top), 143 (bottom right), and 145

Andy Jugle: 58

Lou Koehler: 6 (top), 44–45, 55 (top), 57 (bottom), 101 (bottom), 120–121, 122 (top), 124 (top), 125, and 128 (top left)

National Toy Train Museum/TCA, Strasburg, Pennsylvania: 6 (middle), 8, 11 (both), 14, 16 (bottom), 17 (both), 18 (top), 19 (both), 20, 21, 22, 23 (bottom), 30, 32 (both), 33, 34 (bottom), 35, 36–37, 37 (both), 38 (top), 40 (right), 41, 42, 43 (all), 48–49, 49 (top), 50 (both), 51, 52 (both), 53, 56, 57 (top), 58, 60, 61, 62 (both), 63, 68 (bottom), 92 (top), 93 (all), 96–102 (comic book), 96 (all), 103 (left), 105 (right), 109 (bottom), 111 (top), 115 (top), 119, 122–123 (bottom), 123 (middle left), 134, 138 (right), 143 (bottom left), 144, 146, 150 (bottom)

Jim Patterson: 3, 7 (background), 75 (bottom), 83, 87 (bottom), 92 (bottom left and right), 94, 95 (both), 97 (bottom), 99 (bottom), 100 (bottom), 102 (bottom), 111 (bottom), 112–113 (all), 114 (bottom), 115 (bottom), 124 (bottom right), 132–133, 136 (both), 138 (left), 139, 140 (top), 141 (bottom), 142 (bottom), 147, and 152 (top)

Private Collection: 38–39 (bottom), 55 (bottom), 75 (top), 85, and 86

PAGE 1: Built between 1957 and 1960, this semaphore signal allows two trains to run on the same track by holding up a following train on a dead stretch of track until the preceding train has cleared a safe length. It is controlled by track clips that designate the live and dead stretches of track and is triggered automatically.

PAGE 2: Emerging from a bridge in the light of dawn is a 336 Northern type 4-8-4 steamer (produced between 1953 and 1956). The smoke is not blasting from the locomotive's stack because it is rolling so slowly. This view of the locomotive shows off the wide boiler left over from its O gauge origins.

PAGE 3: Arguably, the Royal Blue is the most elegant American Flyer locomotive. Created in the prewar years to run on three-rail O gauge track, the design looks perfectly at home on S gauge rails. The 4-6-2 Pacific type was based on a photogenic but short-lived Baltimore & Ohio shrouded steamer. Despite its dynamic bullet shape, the 350 Royal Blue never sold well and was generally underpowered for long trains of heavyweight passenger cars. This Model 350 was produced in 1948.

DEDICATION

To our Moms, Gloria and Lillian, who always smiled sweetly when they asked,
"Have you gotten a real job yet?"

ACKNOWLEDGMENTS

Writing about the history of a company that no longer exists is a form of corporate archeology. Instead of working through bone fields with a pick and toothbrush, we dug through reams of yellowed paper, old newsletters, published and unpublished works, catalogs, annual reports, repair manuals, and tape-recorded interviews. In the case of American Flyer, we were writing about two distinct companies run by two strong-willed and visionary entrepreneurs.

W.O. Coleman and A.C. Gilbert were poles apart, yet both were the core motivators of their very unique American Flyer companies. When the health of each failed, their corporate fiefdoms collapsed. But the papers, pictures, and words left behind by these men and their associates clearly trace the arc of their endeavors. The compilation of these illuminating documents fell to American Flyer enthusiasts who made their files available for our research.

Don Heimburger of Heimburger House Publishing opened doors to American Flyer collectors. He introduced us to Andy Jugle, who offered binders filled with corporate data and newsletters dealing with treasured toy train minutiae. Andy loaned us taped interviews and frequently revealed many insights into American Flyer's culture and the fine toy trains they built. His collected remembrances from American Flyer employees are frequently referred to throughout this book.

Our good friends, John V. Luppino and Gary Lavinus at the Train Collectors Association (TCA) in Strasburg, Pennsylvania, made their archive and large toy train collection available to us once again. Specifically, we acknowledge the hard work of Jan Athey, the TCA librarian, who armed us with a stack of photocopies of prewar American Flyer materials. The River Forest, Winnetka, and Oak Park, Illinois, historical societies provided information about William Hafner, W.O. Coleman, and the Coleman family.

We also drew on *A.C. Gilbert's Heritage,* a compilation of articles edited by Don Heimburger; *Famous American Flyer Trains* by Paul C. Nelson (a collection of fourteen years of Nelson's writing in the *S Gaugian* magazine's "American Flyer Collector's Column"), and the available out-of-print Greenberg series of American Flyer books. A.C. Gilbert left behind a body of recollections in his autobiography, *The Man Who Lives in Paradise,* which was reprinted by Heimburger House Publishing in 1990.

Dr. Hillel "Hilly" Lazarus, Historian Emeritus of American Flyer lore, was kind enough to consult his twenty-five-year-old archive to give us one phone number that opened the resource floodgates to the Coleman family. We owe a debt of gratitude to Mrs. Randolph Coleman, Louise S. Coleman-Brown, William L. Coleman, and Mrs. Kirby Coleman Brown for their generous contribution of family photographs, memorabilia, vintage home movies, remembrances, and audiotaped interviews.

We thank the following for generously opening their train layouts for photography: David Avedesian, Bill Bateman, Barry Berson, Monte Heppe, Lou Koehler, and Jim Patterson. Special thanks to the National Toy Train Museum staff and volunteers, including June Aydelotte and Judy Katrinak.

Finally, with all the expert help supporting us, any errors must be ours alone.

CONTENTS

INTRODUCTION

TOP: A Type 16 wind-up loco from 1923 is loaded with cast-on details including rivets, pop valves, an extra dome (in addition to those for sand and steam), and a kerosene-type headlamp that was by then long obsolete on major railroads.
OPPOSITE: This collection reveals the variety of prewar American Flyer passenger cars, ranging from the earliest four-wheel cars to the eight wheelers, all made of stamped steel and most—prior to 1927—decorated with lithography.

The story of American Flyer toy trains is about two companies that failed magnificently. Why are the two companies that built American Flyer trains still discussed, debated over, and written about more than thirty years after the lights were switched off and the last employee walked out the door? Didn't American Flyer compete against Lionel for sixty years and didn't Lionel finally win out? Didn't Lionel buy up what was left of American Flyer in 1967 before Lionel itself went bust?

American Flyer went into the history books as an "also." When General Mills picked up the pieces of Lionel in 1970, the company "also" kept American Flyer. Richard Kughn, the millionaire entrepreneur and train collector, bought the Lionel trademark, lock, stock, and barrel, in 1985, and "also" brought along the American Flyer name. Today, Lionel L.L.C.

"also" grudgingly pushes out a few pieces of S gauge American Flyer through the back door, but even that hand-out is on shaky ground in the current rough-and-tumble toy train marketplace.

What keeps the American Flyer flame flickering when it should be a footnote in history like Carlisle & Finch, Howard, Knapp, Dorfan, and Ives? American Flyer trains are still studied, collected, operated, and replicated because they left us a legacy of some of the finest toy trains ever built. It's really that simple.

In its beginning days, during the early 1900s, American Flyer entertained a lot of boys and girls who might not have been able to afford the big, expensive electric trains. In many rural areas, where there was no electricity, an American Flyer wind-up motor moved the toy train freight on down the line. You can't really call American Flyer's motor "clockworks," because that implies something fussy that belongs in an antique timepiece on the mantel. The rugged Flyer wind-up motor was built for the eight-year-old who wanted a long run out of each tightening of the spring over and over and over again. From mechanical to electric trains, prewar American Flyer locomotives, rolling stock, and accessories were built to last year after year. They were wonderful toys that engaged a kid's imagination from the years of America's awakening before the Great War, during the cultural explosion of the jazz-age 1920s, and through the grim days of the Great Depression.

When you abandoned your wind-up American Flyer set (which was most likely handed down to your little brother or sister) to move on to the real deal, an electric train, you and your friends swapped cars and ran trains on each other's rail-road. Everything—Lionel, Dorfan, Ives, American Flyer—ran on the same three-rail, O gauge track. Even the couplers were designed so a Lionel loco could haul Ives freight cars in a train tailed with an American Flyer caboose. Connections

An example of an exported British Flyer, this 0-4-0, first built in 1915, looks quite European. It has no cowcatcher—a unique American attachment—and is a tank engine carrying its own water and coal supplies for short runs. The GNR—Great Northern Railway—lettering on the water tank is both cast and painted.

AMERICAN

FLYER

10

take on the challenge of running American Flyer. He turned to a man he had known since World War I, when they worked together to establish the Toy Manufacturers of the U.S.A.—Alfred Carlton Gilbert.

A.C. Gilbert had been a hard-charging entrepreneur from the time he stepped into his first pair of long pants. A former Olympic pole-vaulter and the successful inventor of the Erector Set, Gilbert immediately began developing a marketing concept based on "realism," as opposed to Lionel's "unrealistic," sawed-off train models. He chose 3/16-inch (0.48cm)-to-the-foot (0.3m) scale and began turning out new tooling to create scale-model trains that could run on three-rail, O gauge track. The new locos looked great and ran well. In the spring of 1939, W.O. Coleman died at age forty-seven. Then on December 7, 1941, America went to war and all toy train building stopped. Everything changed at American Flyer.

After the war, those 3/16-inch (0.48cm) scale-model trains came out running on S gauge, two-rail track. Gilbert had carried his "realism" agenda to the next logical step. Many American Flyer scholars have pondered this question: if Gilbert had returned to the marketplace with three-rail, O gauge track, would American Flyer trains still be sought-after today, alongside MTH, K-Line, Weaver, Atlas O, Williams Electric Trains, and others for a share of the market? We'll never know, but Gilbert did succeed in offering toy train operators a clear choice between trains that could and could not run on their friends' three-rail, O gauge tracks.

The War of the Gauges was waged for twenty-two years. Lionel outspent, outpromoted, and outproduced American Flyer. Yet, American Flyer developed a solid following for its trains, which looked better, cost less, and ran on two-rail track, just like the real thing. But kids with American Flyer trains could no longer swap cars with their Lionel pals, or run on each other's railroads. They joined American Flyer clubs and responded to Gilbert's seemingly endless promotional gimmicks. Some of them even won trips to tour the famous Gilbert Hall of Science in New York. A sense of having something better than the run-of-the-mill Lionel became the philosophy propounded by American Flyer marketers against Lionel's drumbeat of two-rail put-downs.

that didn't work terribly well were fixed with a piece of string. Millions of kids got rug burns on their knees from hours of playing with these wonderful toys.

With all things fairly equal, how do we separate the winners from the losers? In time, Dorfan's die-casting alloy began to crack and its production processes required too much handwork. The Depression sank the New Jersey–based company. Ives designed some of the best toy trains ever built, but its management and bookkeeping were so sloppy the company stopped turning a profit. The Depression sank Ives, too. American Flyer and Lionel went in together and bought what remained of Ives. But it turned out that the two bosses, William Ogden Coleman of American Flyer and Joshua Lionel Cowen of Lionel, detested each other. American Flyer bought its way out of the deal and limped through the 1930s, waging war against Lionel with words and promotions and more exceptional new trains.

But Lionel was better at promotions, more ruthless in its advertising, and had deeper pockets. By the end of the 1930s, Coleman was sick and the luster had faded from the American Flyer lines. Coleman needed someone who could

A.C. Gilbert died in 1961 and his son, who took over the company upon his father's death, died in 1963. By the end of the 1960s, both Lionel and American Flyer were in ruins. America's railroads had begun their decline. Electric trains had lost their relevance as toys. In the new, fast-turnaround, chain-store economy, large chunks of American farmland were being paved over and "malled." In the end, American Flyer trains had become sad shadows of their former glory. The same was true of Lionel's pitiful offerings.

Lionel, however, had become a household name—like Coca-Cola or Ford. American Flyer was an iconoclast. The conglomerate economy of the 1970s didn't need iconoclasts; it needed diversified profits. Lionel was rescued. American Flyer became an "also" that trailed along with Lionel's barrels and boxes of assets.

But a hard core of American Flyer collectors and scholars remained faithful to those wonderful trains. As the history of the toy train industry evolved, their loyalty to the concepts underlying American Flyer has been vindicated. Scale models are replacing the traditional toy trains. There is room for low-cost, high-quality trains alongside the high-volume, high-profile offerings.

Collectible American Flyer trains continue to run on their two-rail, tinplate track. Wheels, motor parts, and accessories are available from a number of suppliers. Clubs and newsletters keep everyone in the American Flyer family in touch, as that great toy train legacy lives on.

In the chapters that follow, we'll examine the two companies that created the American Flyer mystique, looking at the trains themselves, as well as the people who designed, built, and sold them. We'll show why the American Flyer of today has transcended its lowly position as Lionel's poor cousin. Or, in the words of A.C. Gilbert, "Hello, boys! Have we got a surprise for you!"

CHAPTER ONE

COLEMAN'S HALSTED STREET TRAIN FACTORY

When American Flyer published its first catalog of toy trains in 1910, the fastest vehicle known to man was the steam locomotive. It was also the biggest and the noisiest, and almost every kid in the country wanted to be a railroad engineer. A passenger flier, with smoke firing from its stack like artillery blasts, hammered through a rural road crossing at speeds more than one hundred miles per hour (161kph), valve gear churning, fire box glowing cherry red, and whistle shrieking. The ground shook, horses got spooked, and sparks flew as it faded into the distance, leaving a swirling cloud of marvelously pungent coal smoke in its wake. All that power and speed were under the control of one man at the throttle. Every young boy wanted a toy train set so he could control the throttle of his own locomotive. By 1910, there were plenty of miniature trains to choose from—depending on how much money Dad brought home in his paycheck.

The rich kids got fancy German trains from Marklin, Carette, and Bing, or big trains that ran on track two inches (5cm) wide from Carlisle & Finch, the Knapp Electrical & Novelty Company, the Howard Miniature Lamp Company, and the Lionel Manufacturing Corporation. For kids who lived in areas with no electricity—and there were a lot of them in rural areas—and kids whose parents didn't have twenty dollars to spare for a train set, there were locomotives powered by a wind-up motor. The Ives Manufacturing Corporation, which had been in the toy business since the end of the Civil War, built the best American wind-up, or "mechanical," train sets. They had crammed a sturdy gear and pawl motor together with a long, flat,

coiled-steel spring into a cast-iron locomotive with cast-iron wheels. A start/stop lever on the loco was the throttle and the brake—until the spring ran down and the New York to Chicago Flier had to be rewound (somewhere near Cleveland).

A small line of wind-up toy trains had been produced since 1900 by a Chicago company owned by William F. Hafner. That's where our American Flyer story begins.

Born in Chicago in 1870, William Hafner started his working career as a box broker. Before the days of disposable cardboard boxes, everything was shipped and handled in wooden boxes and barrels. Once the merchandise was unpacked, the wooden crates and barrels were sold to someone like Hafner who, in turn, resold them to other shippers. Hafner, who also liked to tinker, designed a simple, but reliable, spring-powered wind-up motor in his spare time. Around 1900 he began using this small motor to power a miniature stake-bed truck and a small toy lawn swing. The following year, about the time personal gasoline-powered buggies were beginning to putt-putt around Chicago streets, he started the Hafner Company and built a small sheet-metal automobile called the Hafner Roundabout. Seven inches (18cm) in length, with a cloth seat, it resembled the latest experiment in gas buggy technology by Ransom E. Olds, right down to the steering tiller. The Hafner Roundabout's wheels were fixed into one of nineteen grooves that allowed it to travel straight or in a fixed-radius turn. With one wind-up, the spring was powerful enough to drive the car one hundred feet (30m).

The little car was a big success, so in 1903, W.F. Hafner and Company was incorporated with 374 shares of common stock. Along with his partner, William Crawford, Hafner set up shop in a factory at 19 South Canal Street in Chicago. In the winter of that same year, Hafner and his wife, Addie, left their home in Oak Park, Illinois, to travel to California for her health. Their son, Robert, stayed behind to spend the holidays with his grandmother. On Christmas morning, young Robert came downstairs to find an Ives wind-up train set ready to circle the decorated tree.

A look at that train set when he returned from California might have given Hafner the idea of building wind-up trains of his own, because by 1906, his factory was turning out a

small quantity of cast-iron, wind-up trains that were sold right in Chicago. His son now had train track that ran down the home's long hallway, where whizzing Hafner locomotives carried local passengers from Livingroomville to East Diningroom with a stop at Parlortown for coal and water.

Disaster struck as Christmas of 1906 drew near. William Hafner came down with typhoid fever; during his long recovery, his toy train business foundered. He was acquainted with Chicago businessman W.O. Coleman, who was the owner of the Edmonds-Metzel Hardware Company, a manufacturer of wrenches and paring knives. Hafner wanted to build his toy trains at the Edmonds-Metzel plant; in return, Coleman would receive a share of the profits.

William Ogden Coleman was born in Rockford, Illinois, on January 1, 1864, the first child of John S. Coleman and Julia Camman Coleman. He grew up answering to the nickname, "Will." The Coleman family, which was quite large, had migrated west from New York in 1851, settling in the Midwest. Will's mother, Julia, died of heart failure in 1876 at age thirty-seven. Five years later, when Will was seventeen, he left for Chicago. Within a year he was working for the Burley and Tyrrell China Company, but living near the store close to Lake Michigan was hard on his sinuses, so he moved in with his sister, Elizabeth Patterson, in Oak Park.

Will Coleman sold Burley and Tyrrell china dishware on the road until 1889, and then went to work in the store. On Thanksgiving day in 1891, he married Anna May Crenshaw and they both moved in with Elizabeth. Anna May gave birth to a son, William Ogden Coleman Jr., on November 18, 1892. The boy would be called "Ogden." Shortly thereafter, the Colemans moved to a house of their own in River Forest, Illinois.

The senior Coleman was a hard worker and a sharp businessman, rising to full partner and the position of vice president of Burley and Tyrrell by 1900. At age forty-two, Will Coleman had expanded his business interests to include his buy-out of the Edmonds-Metzel Hardware Company. The company was not doing well and needed a new product. In response to William Hafner's proposal to build wind-up toy trains, Coleman told Hafner that if a sizable order for these toy trains could be put on the table, they had a deal.

AMERICAN

FLYER

NATION
WIDE
LINES
REFR. LINE
M.C.L.R.8677
NATION
WIDE
LINES
HAMS&BACON
SPECIALTIES

TOP: Two-year-old William Ogden Coleman III, with a playmate, sends an American Flyer wind-up loco and passenger car on its journey around a loop of track in 1919. Despite his youthful immersion in the world of toy trains, Ogden Coleman's first son opted not to follow his father into the toy train business.

RIGHT: The American Flyer Manufacturing Company helped this little tyke's imagination along with the 1915 catalog cover showing a smoke-belching steamer in place of the little wind-up toy train.

After packing up a box with a sample of his train and track, Hafner traveled to the offices of New York toy distributor Steinfeld Brothers. The executives at Steinfeld liked what they saw and wrote up an order for fifteen thousand dollars worth of trains. Hafner returned, put the order on Coleman's desk, and they shook hands. Coleman's main source of income still came from Burley and Tyrrell. He was also a member of the Chicago Athletic Club, the very swank South Shore Country Club, and was one of the earliest members of the Chicago Automobile Club. His business and social calendar was crowded. He knew nothing about building and marketing toys, so he left the operation of the toy train line to William Hafner, agreeing that Hafner would eventually receive a larger share of the profits if the company was successful.

Coleman watched the 1907 line of wind-up toy trains sell very well; by contrast, the market for his hardware took a nosedive.

Let's take a look at the trains that were becoming so popular in the Windy City. Compared to big electric trains, the little cast-iron puffers took a lot of kid-supplied imagination to become smoke-belching, whistle-screaming steamers hurtling down the main line. There were two locomotives with no catalog numbers and they hauled passenger cars only. Collectors call the first 1907 loco the "No. 1" and its companion the "No. 2." These locos had no front-wheel pilot

truck, four drivers, and no trailing wheel truck (0-4-0) and came with a tin coal tender numbered 328 that coupled with one or two little stamped-steel passenger cars.

There was a three-window car in blue or red with "Pullman" printed above the windows and "Chicago" beneath them. In these cars, neither the windows nor the doors were punched out, and remained white squares. A second model was a bit more deluxe: it came in a variety of colors, the windows were punched out, and the lettering above the windows read "American Flyer." Each car was four-and-a-half inches (11cm) long and rode on four enormous, flanged wheels. The little train used simple, flat-stamped, hook-and-slot couplers that combined both male and female functions.

Hafner's spring motor was speed-governed, so the locos didn't just zip away like a bullet and then slow as the spring wound down. The speed remained more or less constant until a rewind was needed. The main difference between the two locomotives was that the No. 2 had drive rods and

No. 10.   Iron Locomotive, [Speed Regulated, Brake, Hand Rails and Piston Rods], Tender, One Large Car, 8 Pieces Track. . . . .

TOP: The catalog cover and pages from the Edmonds-Metzel catalog showing American Flyer trains as part of the hardware company's offerings. This catalog predates American Flyer's 1910 catalog, which was entirely dedicated to the train line. Shown is the Hafner-designed "No. 2" locomotive, 328 tender, and the earliest version of the "Chicago" passenger car with four windows, offered from 1907 to about 1913.

BOTTOM: The 1907 to 1909 No. 2 American Flyer locomotive designed by William Hafner. There are no drive rods or handrails on this well-worn example, but the loco has the early six-spoke wheels. Hafner engines had the wind-up key on the left.

handrails and, protruding from the rear of the cab, was a brake lever that released or stopped the spring motor. The No. 1 model, by contrast, was a bit stripped down. You wound 'er up and let 'er rip. Each engine came with a set, complete with passenger cars and an oval of sectional two-rail track.

In 1910, Edmonds-Metzel became the American Flyer Manufacturing Company, whose sole business was building the unassuming little wind-up trains in a plant at 1920 West Kinzie Street in Chicago. For three years, Hafner ran the business, doing well in competition with an old-time power-house, the Ives Manufacturing Corporation, which was the industry leader.

Edward Ives had built his toy company into a business legend. By 1901, however, he had become a conservative, old mossback who had been practically bullied into producing a wind-up train that ran on sectional, two-rail track. His thirty-two-year-old son, Harry, looked around and envisioned Ives toy trains running on electricity, while Ives was bragging about the power of the company's coil spring! Under Harry's badgering, Edward the Patriarch relented, and Ives mechanics managed to stuff an electric motor into Ives' largest wind-up loco. For years, Edward Ives had made a point of saying that electric trains were merely a passing fad.

American Flyer's first catalog and newspaper ads, which ran in 1910, offered six train sets, ranging in price from seventy-five cents for an iron loco, tender, one-passenger car, and six lengths of track ("Train will cover the circle about 15 times with one winding," according to the catalog) to $3.50 for a much better loco, tender, three cars, two double switches, more track, and a track crossover. These "improved" American Flyer trains were now gaining shelf space outside Chicago's local market.

In 1913, William Hafner approached Will Coleman to consummate what he considered to be the second part of their initial handshake deal. Hafner expected to receive a bigger share of the now-profitable company. Will Coleman claimed to have no memory of that part of the agreement. Angry with Coleman's apparent double-dealing, Hafner pulled out of American Flyer to form the Hafner Manufacturing Company, building those charming wind-up trains in a plant at 648 Ruby Street in Chicago. The charming little trains rolled out with their keys turning from the Christmas of 1914 until the 1950s.

Prior to 1914 and the start of the Great War in Europe, America was Germany's largest offshore toy market. To "buy German" was to buy quality, well-engineered, and expensive amusements for Junior and Jill. German toy sales had increased from $4 million to $7.8 million by 1910. Many American manufacturers, including American Flyer, had been buying accessories from

TOP: This little four-wheel observation car represents a vast group of 1107 passenger cars dating from 1914. It is made of stamped steel with the details lithographed on the surface. This particular car was manufactured in 1931 in the Halsted Street plant.
BOTTOM: A fanciful scene on the cover of the 1910 American Flyer catalog was designed to fire up young imaginations. In that year, the American Flyer Manufacturing Company was established, producing cast-iron wind-up trains at the Edmonds-Metzel Manufacturing plant.

RIGHT: An advertisement from 1915 shows a well-dressed lad caressing his Flyer passenger car alongside copy touting the "wreck-less train." The ad guarantees the superior quality of steel pinions (over old-fashioned brass) in the wind-up motor. The trains were being built at the Halsted Street factory by this time.

OPPOSITE: American Flyer's Hummer line of low-cost train sets featured locomotives made of stamped steel and devoid of all details except rudimentary suggestions of the basics. The sets were available well into the 1930s. This is an upscale Hummer Type 3 loco featuring handrails.

German-based Bing and other importers. World War I shut down German toy imports into the United States; as a result, American toy makers rushed in to fill the vacuum. Will Coleman saw the opportunities and turned over the reins of American Flyer to his twenty-one-year-old son, Ogden. The match was a natural one. Young Ogden had grown up riding horses in rural River Forest, but developed a mechanic's flair for tinkering with the handmade automobiles of the period. He also enjoyed driving the fast new ones.

Curiously, one of the first things young Ogden did when he took over was move the turning key in the side of every American Flyer locomotive from the left side to the right side. He also changed Hafner's green stripe, painted under the cab windows, to a red stripe.

By 1916, anyone who could read was aware that the United States was being drawn into the European war. America's toy manufacturers decided to form a "unifying" organization—in effect, an old-fashioned boys' club—that would help stabilize the toy market when Germany was cut off altogether. The toy train community was close knit. The Hafners and the Colemans remained civil on social occasions, despite the falling out over the men's joint business venture. Both of Hafner's sons, Robert and John, were friends with Ogden Coleman.

When the toy manufacturers got together and formed the Toy Manufacturers of the U.S.A., the first president was a dashing young entrepreneur, doctor, and former Olympic pole-vaulter who made a pile of money by creating the Mysto Manufacturing Company—the largest maker of magic tricks in the world—and inventing the Erector Set in 1913. Alfred Carlton Gilbert was a model for the aggressive go-getter of his time. William Hafner and Ogden Coleman were members of the association, and Harry Ives assumed the president's mantel for three years when A.C. Gilbert stepped down.

From 1914 through 1918, American Flyer wind-up toy trains were tinkered with—larger locos and smaller ones were designed and produced. Wider bands on the boiler replaced thinner ones. In 1915, American Flyer introduced a really low-priced "Hummer" line, with a loco made of stamped steel that towed the green No. 513 tender with "Hummer" stamped in yellow on the rear. One thing the

company never did manage to build was a wind-up motor that could go in reverse.

It is likely that Coleman's American Flyer company joined the Hafner Manufacturing Company in buying iron locomotive castings from the Susquehanna Casting Company in Pennsylvania. From 1917 through to the end of the war, there was a shortage of iron for casting. Thanks to lobbying by the Toy Manufacturers of the U.S.A., the shortage didn't affect toy manufacturers during World War I. The next world war, however, brought all toy train production to a screeching halt for five years.

By the end of World War I in 1918, the move to electric trains could be put off no longer: American Flyer's No. 15 cast-iron, wind-up loco had an electric motor stuffed inside and was released as the Model 1225. It ran on three-rail

track, one and a quarter inches (3.2cm) wide, that Ives and Lionel had pioneered, and was available with or without an operating headlight recessed in the smoke box. The train set came with the No. 120 tender, the No. 1105 baggage car with sliding doors, and two No. 1106 passenger cars riding on more prototypical four-wheel trucks. Eight sections of curved track, four sections of straight rails, and either a transformer or three battery hook-ups with the No. 1251 controlling rheostat completed the package. American Flyer was playing catch-up with its two main rivals, Ives and Lionel.

Joshua Lionel Cowen had already bitten the bullet in 1910 when, at age twenty-nine, he had proposed selling Lionel to Edward Ives, only to be rebuffed. In 1912, Ives had released the No. 3240 electric locomotive that ran on the company's "1 gauge" track. This locomotive was modeled after the New York Central S-Motor electrics, used to haul trains into smoke-free New York City. Shortly thereafter, Ives built the 7000 line of freight cars. Lionel had been committed to its large Standard gauge trains, but realized that the company needed a smaller, less costly line to compete with Ives. In 1915 Lionel released its own line of "O gauge" trains, also modeled after the S-Motor prototype. Neither Lionel nor Ives built electric-powered steam locomotives until 1930.

AMERICAN

FLYER

22

The year 1918 marked another milestone in American Flyer history, one that ended one era and began another. On November 30, Will Coleman paid a visit to the Oak Park Country Club, where he took advantage of unseasonably warm weather to play twenty-four holes of golf. Later that afternoon, he took a stroll with his wife, Anna May, on Park Avenue near Lake Street in River Forest. They were going to take a streetcar into town to have dinner. Suddenly, he fell dead on the street. He was fifty-four years old. His son Ogden, at age twenty-six, became the sole owner of the American Flyer Manufacturing Company.

LEFT TOP: Rowena Coleman holds her first son, William Ogden Coleman III, alongside her husband, twenty-five-year-old William Ogden Coleman Jr., in 1918—the year that marked the start of his reign at American Flyer.

RIGHT TOP: By 1918, the "winged locomotive" logo had been established. This catalog shows a wind-up set complete with turntable, tunnel, and semaphore signals. "The Toy for the Boy" left no doubt as to the targeted market for toy trains.

BOTTOM: A six-and-a-half-inch (16.5cm) baggage car numbered 1104 is a charming addition to any Flyer passenger train. These cars were first offered in 1910 and were available until World War I. American Flyer was constantly tinkering with color schemes, which drives collectors quite mad today.

AMERICAN

FLYER

CHAPTER TWO

AMERICAN FLYER ROARS INTO THE 1920s

As the volatile 1920s made their mark on America, W.O. Coleman Jr., called "Ogden" by most people, had a firm grip on the company he inherited in 1918 from his father. By 1919, American Flyer had introduced its first electric train sets. The models 1200 and 1225 cast-iron, steam-type locomotives headed Pullman passenger cars, each riding on four wheels. The iron shells were cast in Pennsylvania and shipped to the American Flyer plant at 2219 South Halsted Street in Chicago. The cast-iron, and later sheet-metal, wind-up locos would share Flyer catalog pages with the electric lines well into the 1930s.

Interestingly, American Flyer chose to enter the electric train market with cast-iron steam engines in 1919. Most collectors assume steamers were chosen because real steam locomotives were a familiar sight to the local Chicago market. It was also more cost-effective for American Flyer to cram an electric motor into its largest cast-iron, seven-inch (18cm), wind-up loco than to design and build any other engine from scratch. Through the years, American Flyer stayed with cast iron for its wind-up line, continually upgrading the quality and detail of the castings. The Model 16 wind-up locomotive, built in 1921 and cataloged in 1922, is a good case in point.

The toylike, single-dome locos had grown into hefty engines, seven inches (18cm) in length, studded with rivets and other realistic details. The Model 16 actually has too many rivets and one dome too many (unless the extra dome represents a second sand dome, but that's unlikely, since there are no sand pipes running from it to the drivers). A dual air compressor is also cast into its left side, together with additional piping and walkways. There is a bump on

PREVIOUS PAGES: This model 4687 is the original 1927 Wide gauge version of the Improved President's Special. Its Rolls Royce Blue paint job with nickel and brass trim hints at future "improved" models. There are front and back lights, a bell just off-center, and a pair of nickel air tanks added to each side of the black frame.

OPPOSITE: Pulling its passenger train into the station late into the night, this 1218 S-motor type locomotive rolls past patient passengers. This 1920s engine was a familiar sight in New York stations since smoke-puffing steam engines were prohibited from entering NYC terminals. Note the straplike Type 2 handrails and huge headlight. When electric lights were added to cars and accessories, running toy trains in a dark room became a magical experience.

top of the boiler, directly in front of the cab, that appears to stand in for the safety-valve cluster and headlight turbocharger normally found there. One real anomaly is the square headlight affixed to the front of the smoke box. It is a kerosene-type that, by the 1920s, was found only on back water short lines, where antique locos from the nineteenth century were one jump away from the scrap heap. All in all, the Model 16 has a distinct, "railroady" look to it.

A spring-driven motor, larger than that used in previous smaller engines, powered the locomotive's four fourteen-spoke wheels. Between the front drivers was a small lever that serves as an "automatic stop" device. A trip wire raised between the rails at the desired stop point triggered this feature. The loco whizzed up to the trip, then stopped dead, banging together the passenger cars and killing everyone on board. Reaching into the cab with a finger and lifting the release lever freed the gears. Another lethal feature of the Model 16 was the right-hand threads on the drive wheels. Instead of tightening the wheels as the loco moved forward—as with left-hand threads—the steamer occasionally unthreaded a powered front drive wheel, sending the train thrashing onto the carpet and, yet again, killing all passengers and crew on board.

The Model 16, with its large key turning in its right side, remained in the American Flyer lineup until 1930. By that time, it had been painted bright red and marketed to little kids who didn't know steam engines were really supposed to be black.

As Prohibition, hot jazz, fast cars, and even faster flappers changed the tenor of American life, Ogden Coleman moved American Flyer into direct competition with Ives and Lionel. In 1920, he reached for a broader market by introducing the four-wheel Models 1201, 1217, and 1218 electric-type locomotives. These stamped-steel engines resembled the steeple cab "S-Motors" used in New York and all along the East Coast as well as a Michigan Central terminal loco prototype. Lionel had entered the O gauge market back in 1915, producing these electric types exclusively. The only steam engines built by Lionel ran on its large Standard gauge track.

These early Flyer electrics were hardly things of beauty. The 1201, which only came in black with red window trim,

was rubber-stamped with "American Flyer Lines" and "Motor 1201." The eight-inch (20cm) engine had no headlight or pantographs and was studded with rivets. Its sole claim to decoration was a set of nickel handrails. The Model 1217 was a bit more with it, offering a new color, brown, and, in 1921, dark green in addition to black. Over the six-year lifetime of the Model 1218, the range of colors extended to orange, red, maroon, and dark blue.

These humble little electrics were the first in a line that would culminate with the finest locomotives American Flyer ever built. And with their appearance, all design of new steam models stopped. The cast-iron 1225 steamer and a close cousin, the Model 1216, stayed in the catalog until 1924. The electric locos, made of stamped steel, could be manufactured in the Halsted Street plant, allowing expansion of the Flyer line at minimal cost. Lionel and Ives had already used that formula successfully, and Ogden Coleman, if anything, was a cost-conscious manufacturer.

The mid-1920s marked the end of American Flyer's production of cheap trains, called the "Hummer" sets. At one time or another, most toy train manufacturers offered really low-cost train sets. Lionel sold its "Winner" line with its own catalog and very little mention of the Lionel name. Those trains went on to become "Lionel Jr." sets and finally Lionel "Scout," and the O27 gauge trains that we have today. In 1915, American Flyer launched the "Hummer" line, which did not carry the American Flyer name.

Hummer locomotives, with Nos. 1 through 3, were minimalist wind-up affairs, cobbled together out of sheet metal with no side rods or brakes. They towed smaller, four-wheel tenders and a variety of four-wheel Hummer passenger cars. By 1925, the Hummer line had lost out to snazzier models and low-cost "New York Express" cast-iron locos started taking over hauling the toylike passenger cars, renamed the Empire Express. Those dinky little cars lasted until the mid-1930s, around the time when the last wind-up locomotives were retired.

The mid-1920s were a time of significant change for American Flyer, as Ogden and his engineers and designers pursued a larger customer base alongside Lionel, Ives, and a new hard-charging builder of die-cast locos named Dorfan,

AMERICAN

FLYER

LIKE FATHER, LIKE SON

William Ogden Coleman Jr. was truly his father's son when it came to hedging his bets. While he was president of the American Flyer Manufacturing Company, he also was a partner in a laundry machine company in Freeport, Illinois. Sales representatives for American Flyer carried more than train samples in pursuit of a buck. They sold a line of Structo toys, cars, and trucks to compete with the popular toy manufacturer, Buddy L. These toys were built in the Freeport plant and displayed in the American Flyer catalog. Coleman also invested in a lithography company—the Metal Lithography and Coating Company—that provided car sides and decorated accessories for Flyer until 1928, when the company shifted over to sprayed-on enamel paint for its rolling stock.

Other Coleman-produced products included a toy cash register that rang up each sale and printed a receipt; an American Flyer Typewriter "with CAPITAL and Small Letters" that, as the catalog promised, "makes a game out of homework"; and a little trolley car for the Chicago Century of Progress in 1933. Toy airplanes, with props driven by chain linkage to the wheels, were pushed across carpets, while Little Billy or Betty rode an Ingo bike on the sidewalk. An Ingo bike was a strange two-wheeler that operated when children pressed their weight down on the narrow platform between the front and rear wheels, then eased up, causing a spring drive to turn the rear wheel. Hopping up and down on this bike to move forward was supposed to become a "national craze," according to the dealer ads. Offered in "Junior," "Juniorette," and "Senior" sizes, this curious specimen, built by the Steel and Disc Division of Chicago's Borg Warner Corporation, somehow never caught on.

If Ogden had a few moments in between wheeling and dealing to ponder his next acquisition, he might have wished to taste once again the sweet apples from his Dad's former fruit orchard in Moser, Oregon. Will Coleman had bought an apple orchard in Oregon from a Burley and Tyrrell salesman. It was located about twelve miles (19km) from Mount Hood near the town of Moser, Oregon. He had named the orchard "Marjowanna," after his family: "Mar" was for his daughter Margaret, "J" stood for second daughter Julia, "W" was Will's letter, and "Anna" was for his wife, Anna May. When Will Coleman died in 1918, Ogden decided to sell Marjowanna Farm. After the sale, a barrel of apples arrived at the Coleman house.

William Ogden Coleman Jr. (far left) sits next to his grandfather, John Coleman (who holds great-grandson William Ogden Coleman III), and his father, William Ogden ("Will") Coleman Sr., circa 1917.

run by two brothers, Milton and Julius Forchheimer. Of all American toys at the time, the electric train was the most complex, comprised the most parts, combined the largest variety of technologies, and relied on huge-volume sales to make up for its largely seasonal appeal. To keep that appeal alive, American toy train manufacturers fought bitterly over every patented advance that might give them a slight edge over their competitors. In 1927, the big edge was a remote-control reverse feature.

Until W.B. Sparks invented the sequence switch, which allowed toy train aficionados to reverse an electric loco's direction from the transformer-throttle position, young conductors had to scoot across the carpet and flip a switch on the loco by hand to make it go in reverse. For once in its life, Ives guessed right and got exclusive rights to use Sparks' patent. Joshua Cowen put the lash to his Lionel engineers to work around that patent, just as Ogden Coleman spurred his designers to do the same. Sparks' system called for a ratchet and pawl, powered by a solenoid that operated a drum reverse switch every time the current was turned off and on. The settings were forward-off-backward-off, operated by a button near the transformer. The "off" acted as a neutral position to eliminate most accidental reverses caused by a power interruption.

Lionel added a simple toggle switch, triggered by a solenoid, to change from forward to reverse. American Flyer used the motor itself to operate the reverse switch.

Unfortunately, on Lionel and American Flyer locos, any power interruption reversed the engine, which caused vast damage and, of course, once again, killed all passengers on board. When Ives went bust in the early 1930s, Lionel and American Flyer joined forces to scoop up that valuable patent along with whatever tinwork, nuts, and bolts were left of the venerable old toy maker.

As with the valuable reverse switch, success in the toy train market relied on beating out, or at least keeping up with, the competition. Ogden Coleman looked at the growing American economy and soaring stock market in the mid-1920s and took a flyer of his own. He committed American Flyer to building really big Wide gauge trains.

Lionel had been dominating the market since 1906 with trains running on track two and one-eighth inches (5.4cm) wide. Other track at that time was two inches (5cm) wide. Lionel scored a marketing coup by calling its track "Standard gauge," thereby rendering all other track gauges "nonstandard." In 1921, Ives abandoned its No. 1 gauge (one and three-quarter inches [4.5cm] between the rails) for the two-and-one-eighth-inch [5.4cm] gauge, calling the new Ives track "Wide Gauge."

American Flyer followed suit and launched its Wide gauge line in the 1925 catalog. An advertisement on page 437 of *The Youth's Companion* of 1925 enticed readers with the following teaser: "Have you seen the big American Flyer Wide Gauge electric train? . . . It sure is a bear!" With drum

Clicking across a stretch of contemporary three-rail O gauge track is an American Flyer Model 1218 (in black with red window frames) from the early 1920s. These four-wheel electrics were of "steeple-cab" design, resembling NYC S-Motor prototypes. This model has wide Type 2 handrails and lots of rivets. Trailing behind is a train consisting of three 1206-type passenger cars with rounded roofs and lithographed details.

AMERICAN

FLYER

TOURING THE 1920s CHICAGO PLANT

While Lionel moved its plant from New York City to New Haven, Connecticut, and then to Irvington, New Jersey, Coleman's American Flyer stayed put near the south side of Chicago. Thanks to Dr. Ed Bernard's tape-recorded interview of a conversation with Maury Romer, a former American Flyer sales engineer, we can virtually tour the plant. The following is a summary of Romer's Recollection.

Down on the sixth floor, all the locomotives, cars, and accessories were assembled. Motors were built with hand-wound armatures, wheels were pressed into place, and conveyors moved the pieces from workstation to workstation. Finished products were tested and passed on to packaging for the trip to the stock room. Small kick and punch presses clattered as stock boys hustled through the thousands of bins with wheeled carts, gathering parts off the racks for the assembly line.

After entering the small lobby at 2219 South Halsted Street, you found an information window and a couple of benches. The telephone operator behind the window, who acted as receptionist, also managed the switchboard. She called your host on the first floor. Sales, accounting, finance, purchasing, planning, and other administrative offices were all on this floor. After passing these offices down a corridor to your right, you opened a door and were slammed by the noise of thirty punch presses pounding out various locomotive, car, and accessory parts from lengths of sheet steel. Passing through this cacophony and the smell of hot oil and grease, you turned left to find the elevator to the seventh floor. If you turned right, you went past Ernie Finkler's office. He was in charge of shipping and receiving. A large door opened out onto the north end of the loading platform where railroad freight cars on a private spur siding delivered raw materials and picked up finished work. Trucks used the south end of the platform.

A ride up the elevator to the seventh floor brought you to Ogden Coleman's office, where the smell of paint assailed you. The smell came from the paint shop, where parts were sprayed with enamel or Japanned black. (In 1927, American Flyer was shifting from lithography to painting and baking on colors in large ovens.) Here, you could look over the shoulder of head engineer Earl Boisslier to see which new designs were being tested. You could stroll through the model shop, or look at products on display in the company showroom.

Precision tools and dies for the stamping machines were created on the north end of the fifth floor, while all the wind-up trains and spring motors were built at the south end. When there was an overflow, some O gauge cars were also built on the fifth floor.

Both the third and fourth floors housed inventory. One unusual place at the back of the building's fourth floor was a locked cage called the "obsolete" room. The Halsted Street plant backed onto a slip off the Chicago River, built to accommodate fireboats in the industrial district. A window opened onto this slip. Any locomotives, cars, or accessories that had not moved from stock over a period of a couple of years were considered "obsolete" and were deemed to be taking up valuable shelf space. A stockman named Joe had the job of determining which products had to go, and threw them out the window onto the slip. From another window up on the sixth floor, locomotives sent in for service that weren't

Opposite: American Flyer made its Wide gauge train sets in a variety of styles. This lower-cost New York Central–style box-cab electric, the 1928 Model 4654, hauled a passenger set called The Statesman.

Top: This postcard shows the exterior of the American Flyer Manufacturing plant in Chicago, circa 1920. Trolleys ran down Halsted Street and a covered rail siding fed boxcars into the plant's loading dock. A lumber slip off the Chicago River to the south (right) ran behind the factory. The plant was once the largest toy train manufacturing facility in the country.

thought to be worthy of repair were also thrown out the window (and new trains were returned to the customer). Parts that were ruined in the manufacturing process, such as armatures wound in the wrong direction, were subject to the foreman's wrath. To avoid someone getting chewed out, a worker named Lefty had the job of gathering up these blunders—sometimes a thousand or more—and throwing them out the window. After twenty years of American Flyer manufacturing, it was amazing that the fireboats could still sail down the slip without running aground on rusty Flyer trains and parts.

At the other end of the fourth floor was the track department. All two-rail track for the wind-up trains and three-rail O gauge track for the electric trains were made here.

By the mid-1920s, the shipping department had moved from the sixth floor to the second floor. There you found a good example of American Flyer thrift—one reminiscent of the days before the Great War. Secondhand crates were purchased from other firms in Chicago, the old labels were steamed off, and American Flyer products were stuffed in, packed tight with paper excelsior. If a dealer wanted twelve trains, track, transformers, and accessories, a picker on the third floor assembled the order and sent all the parts down on a conveyor. The order was laid out on a table. A lad was then sent scurrying into the crate storage room to find a box into which all the products would fit. The nailed-shut crates going out passed parcel post coming in with trains and parts that needed repair. All repair orders were written up on the second floor and then sent up to Lefty to see if they were destined to go out the window or to be fixed.

Finally, the tour ended in the basement, where heavy-duty shearing machines cut up steel sheets into different widths, and a huge MacDonald punch press cut out wheel cups for various train sizes. A

freight elevator carried the barrels of wheels up to the sixth floor for assembly.

The Halsted Street building no longer stands, but you can imagine enterprising kids sitting in a rowboat in that Chicago River slip, holding a sturdy net at the end of a long pole and waiting to see what treasures Joe or Lefty might toss out the window.

TOP: Every American Flyer wind-up locomotive was tested three times before being passed to the packaging and shipping departments.
BOTTOM: Pulling out all the stops in 1928, the American Flyer catalog touts the "Rainbow Line" of electric and wind-up trains, shows a prototypical electric locomotive running through pine forests, and caps it all with the American eagle looking somewhat belligerent.
OPPOSITE: The 3186 center-cab St. Paul–type electric locomotive saw service between 1928 and 1929. It sports brass handrails and a gaudy paint scheme of tan, green, and red. This O gauge four-wheeler is ten and a half inches (26.5cm) long with cropped pilots front and rear. The locos hauled either freight or passenger consists.

rolls and whoop-de-doo, the American Flyer Model 4019 box-cab electric rolled onto dealers' shelves.

This "EXACT COPY of the LATEST New York Central 'TWENTIETH CENTURY LOCOMOTIVE,' " also called "the NEW Wide Gauge 'FEATURE TRAIN,' " was a modest 0-4-0 box cab at the head end of one baggage and two passenger cars (Set 1434) along with a handful of accessories and track. The train was painted maroon.

American Flyer really beat the drum for its Wide gauge line. The company had created a contest for the best "Backyard Railroad," asking kids to create a layout and photograph it to win prizes. Now, the big Wide gauge trains could be included, featuring their "non-rustable" track. Advertisements proclaimed, "The Boys of America Designed This Train!" As 1926 arrived, American Flyer had three lines of toy trains—wind-up, O gauge, and Wide gauge—selling to more enthusiastic children than ever before.

If O gauge train sets were found in homes with a Model A Ford in the driveway and a Victrola record player in the parlor, then kids who played with Standard gauge trains rode in a Packard Eight and listened to an Atwater-Kent radio in the drawing room. The big trains were for the prime rib–eating rich boys. American Flyer had jumped into what today's collectors call the "Classic Period" of toy trains, which lasted from 1923 to 1939. Following Flyer's introduction of the 4000 and 4019 sets, the company introduced an expanded Wide gauge line in 1926. German toy train manufacturers Bing and Marklin offered their own big trains that ran on Standard gauge track. Everyone was determined to come up with a product line that appealed to customers with deep pockets.

American Flyer chose a patriotic theme for its Wide gauge trains, calling its first two sets the All American Limited, hauled by the 4019, and the Sesqui-Centennial Special (named for the 1926 one-hundred-fiftieth anniversary of the Declaration of Independence), pulled by the less expensive Model 4000. Also in 1926, a more elaborate version of the 4019 was offered, named the President's Special. It sported some nickel trim and grommets for flags on the roof. Great hoopla accompanied American Flyer's

TOP: This folded and tabbed watchman's tower from the years 1924–1934 is made of stamped and lithographed steel. A dinging bell to help manage O gauge rail traffic is located below the towerman's shack, which is illuminated by a single bulb. **BOTTOM:** Any kid who found a string of these Wide gauge passenger cars under the mansion's Christmas tree in 1929 had to be impressed. This Model 4393 diner car labeled the "Indianapolis" sports six-steel trucks with brass journals and an on/off switch for interior lighting where the prototype's battery box would be located. Note the brass inset windows and diaphragm on the car's end. The red wheels are just a hoot.

announcement of the train's 1926 debut as reproduced in the American Flyer newsletter *The Collector*:

> The President's Special is our conception of a real train designed and built especially for the President's use. The train was not designed by us alone. It was built from blue prints [sic] furnished us by the New York Central Railroad and the Pullman Car Company and embodies creations and refinements far in advance of those built into ordinary electric trains. Possessing a large locomotive with larger, more luxurious coaches all of which are beautifully finished in a striking shade of buff. As this big, six-foot train lighted with eleven individual electric lights travels along its 20 feet of track it presents an appearance that arouses the admiration of both young and old.

In 1926, American Flyer needed to expand the "playability" of its line of big trains by adding freight cars. The Halsted Street plant was busy cranking out the new passenger sets, so the company turned to Lionel and bought some crates of four No. 10 series freight cars: the 4007 sand car, the 4005 stock car, the 4008 box car, and the 4011 caboose. Standardization of gauge allowed this kind of rolling stock swapping. The companies frequently bought accessories from each other as well. In the catalog that featured the President's Special set, a Lionel crossing gate and automatic train control are also for sale. In the case of the Lionel freight cars, only the couplers proved to be a bit of a problem. The Lionel hook was a bit too wide for the slot in an American Flyer loco's coupler. A few swipes with a file took care of that.

The 1927 Improved President's Special rumbled forth in considerable splendor and to much fanfare. The main box was unchanged from the 4019 concept, but the trim-and-wheel arrangement was significantly different. Clicking along the wide track in a hue of brilliant blue, the big 4687 locomotive now featured a pair of brass pantographs, a bell, and its dual headlights. Four-wheel pilot and trailing trucks were added, together with sand boxes, air tanks under the frame,

and brass journal boxes all around. Following the loco was a set of bright blue passenger cars, riding on six-wheel, brass-trimmed trucks. Underbody detail included a battery box and air tanks. The observation car sported brass gating and a lighted name drumhead on its stern, fit for any president's whistle-stop tour.

The 4687 also made use of American Flyer's "Triple Action Remote Control," its version of a sequence-reverse system. With all these extras, the new sets edged into the $100 price range. AF's competition was stiff. Lionel had its exceptional 402 and 408E electric locomotives, coupled to interior-detailed passenger cars. Dorfan, Ives, and Lionel were all preparing their innovative trains for Christmas 1928. There were a lot of chips on the table.

American Flyer's President's Special for 1926 became The Chief in 1927, while a less expensive and smaller Wide gauge loco (twelve inches [30cm] long) was offered, called The Eagle and painted green. A virtually identical, lower-cost set was the orange-painted Commander. But all the while, these models were only an opening shot for American Flyer's

Rolling down a siding, this 4019 Wide gauge locomotive heralded American Flyer's entry into the "big train" market in 1925. It was one of the forerunners of a series of magnificent locomotives and rolling stock that arrived with the Great Depression.

Right: This beautiful Model 95 train station welcomed American Flyer trains to "Flyer City" in 1926 with considerable lithographed detail over stamped steel, and a working crane for added play value.

Opposite Top: One of the most famous American Flyer catalogs, this 1926 edition features the painting commissioned by General Electric, builders of the locomotive pictured, for presentation to the New York Central, which bought the loco for terminal operations.

Opposite Bottom: As on the 1926 catalog, the New York Central prototype electric terminal locomotive rolls toward the reader on the cover this 1927 American Flyer catalog.

NEW YORK CENTRAL LOBBIES AMERICAN FLYER WITH FINE ART

The advertising rhetoric in American Flyer's catalogs didn't spring entirely from a copywriter's mind. When the New York Central Railroad ordered a big multiwheel electric locomotive from General Electric, GE commissioned an oil painting of the loco and train of passenger cars for presentation to New York Central. American Flyer's decision to bring out the President's Special required blueprints, pictures—whatever Flyer engineers needed to reproduce the loco in Wide gauge. The marketing people at New York Central suggested that the oil painting of their terminal loco should be sent to Ogden Coleman to seal the deal to build the New York Central model. The painting so impressed Coleman that it was used on the cover of the 1925 American Flyer catalog, and again in 1926 and 1927.

Following the breakup of the Chicago American Flyer plant in 1938, the painting was crated for its move to New Haven, Connecticut, and upon arrival was forgotten. Later it was discovered by Maury Romer, a retired American Flyer employee. After his death in 1984, the painting went to the Train Collectors Association Museum in Strasburg, Pennsylvania, where it hangs today, valued at several thousand dollars.

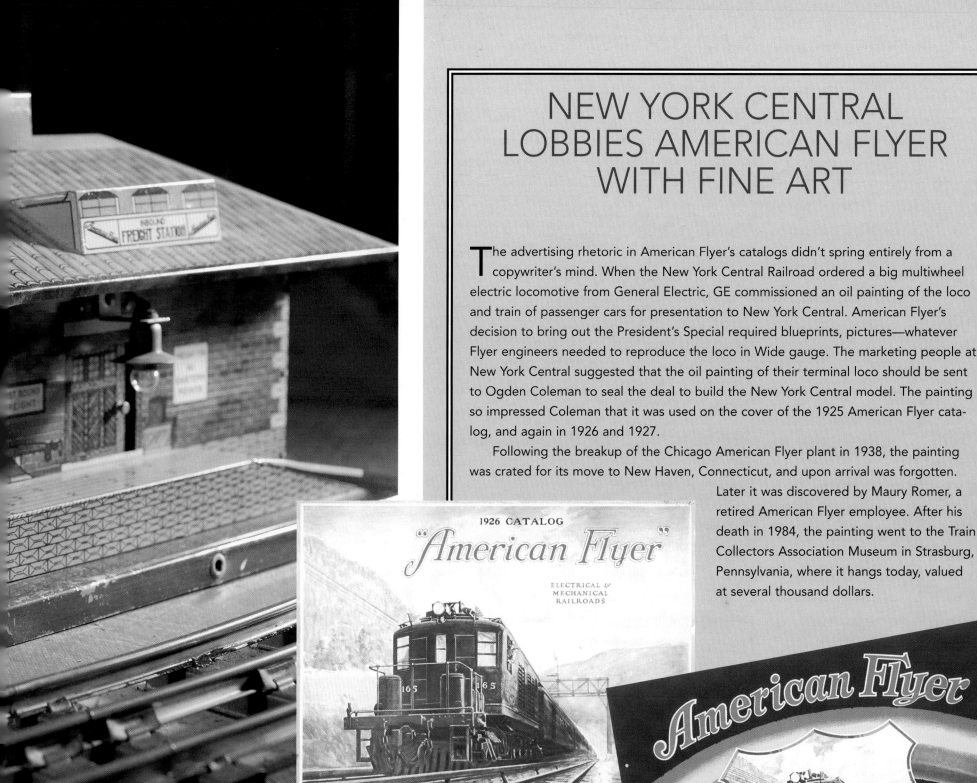

assault on Lionel, Dorfan, and Ives' Wide gauge market share. The precision toolmakers working in the northeast section of the Halsted Street factory's fifth floor had not been idle. The stamping and punch presses on the first floor were working to capacity. There was a definite rumbling sound coming from Chicago.

Many of the great classics of toy train railroading burst on the scene in 1928. Lionel built its largest locomotive to date, the massive 381E, a "St. Paul"–type loco used for heavy hauling up north. It arrived with a train of huge twenty-one-inch (53cm) passenger cars named after states. Dorfan fielded a bright green S-Motor type electric, die-cast with Dorfan Alloy, modeled after the Milwaukee Road's Bi-Polar Olympic locos. It was lavishly trimmed with brass and had so many rivets showing that you could strike a match off its side frames. Ives held the technological edge with its smooth, sequence-reverse system, which all the other companies coveted. But the old toy maker was coughing up red ink from years of bad business decisions and sloppy accounting practices. The bell was tolling for Ives.

American Flyer came out of the blocks in 1928 with an Advanced President's Special, a Shasta Olympic–style electric locomotive, a set of green-and-tan Pocahontas passenger

TOP: Through the 1930s, American Flyer produced many passenger car sets in O gauge. This nine-and-a-half-inch (24cm) observation car riding on Type 8 trucks is typical of the designs.

cars, and a bright red train set called the Hamiltonian, headed by an S-Motor type electric named the Daniel Boone.

Of these Wide gauge offerings, the latest iteration in the President's Special lineage was a dazzler. It was painted "Rolls Royce Blue," with the roof darker than the sides. Besides new trim, including ladders and a chain across the pilot truck, the engine boasted an "Automatic Ringing Bell" as well as the remote reverse sequencer. But it was the gleam of brass that really set the No. 4689 apart.

From the eagle on the front of the pilot truck to the steps, doors, window moldings, journal boxes, air tanks, battery boxes, and ladders, all were shining brass. The pantographs and headlights were crafted in brass, as were the name and number plates. The four cars that made up the Presidential train were also painted two-tone Rolls Royce Blue with brass plates above the windows bearing each car's name: West Point, Academy, Army, Navy, and Annapolis. The lights in each car were controlled by a switch on the car's battery box. Their doors worked, the observation car's platform and marker lights were illuminated, and all the cars clicked along the main on six-wheel, nickel-plated trucks.

Rolling out of the American Flyer shops just behind the Advanced President's Special was the No. 4637 Shasta. An

TOP: Here is the ultimate expression of the President's Special in Wide gauge for 1928. The ends of this big locomotive have been dressed up with red trim on the cowcatcher and sand barrels, a chain has been draped across its front, the handrails above the four-wheel lead truck are nickel, and they are presided over by a wing-spread eagle. The bell on top actually swings in its mounting as the internal bell dings. Brass trim ranges from the journal boxes and air tanks up the ladders, over the battery boxes, past the window frames to the headlights and pantographs on the roof. This gaudy behemoth was (except for the chrome Mayflower) the very top of the line.

BOTTOM: This 1928 catalog cover illustration of the magnificent Wide gauge President's Special locomotive hauling its four illuminated passenger cars through a remote mountain pass fueled the imaginations of many children.

AMERICAN

FLYER

40

easy match for Lionel's huge 381E engine, the Shasta was fifteen inches (38cm) long, trimmed in brass and riding above "Rookie Tan" side frames. Its prototype was a bi-polar electric that ran on the Milwaukee Road's Pacific Extension line to Tacoma, Washington. Brass pantographs, dual head-lights, a bell, and a reverse lever were mounted on the rounded cowlings fore and aft of the center cab. All the doors, handrails, and windows were brass. In addition, a pair of gold-painted castings, representing steps and a fuse box, were affixed to both sides of the cab. Front and rear cow-catchers were bright red, complete with flag holders, and the whole assembly balanced on four wheels.

Trailing behind the Shasta locomotive was a four-car Pocahontas passenger set. These fourteen-inch (36cm) cars glittered with brass trim over their Rookie Tan sides and beneath brown roofs.

The Hamiltonian train followed a New York Central S-Motor type electric, the Daniel Boone, painted red with gray side frames. The 4678 was also encrusted with brass trim. Its passenger cars were essentially the same as the Pocahontas set, except for their bright red color. All these passenger cars rode on four-wheel trucks, studded with brass journal boxes.

Besides some lower-cost versions of the trains already mentioned, American Flyer also promoted its first Wide gauge freight cars in 1928. These were spray-painted with enamel in a rainbow of hues, and oven-dried on the seventh floor of the Halsted Street plant. The gaudy box cars, tank cars, flats, gondolas, and caboose were offered in sets named Trail Blazer and Mountaineer.

Harry Ives decided to call it quits in 1928, as a mountain of debt absorbed all his company's profits. The Ives compa-ny's assets were put on the block. Lionel and American Flyer teamed up to buy what was left of Ives and—besides finally getting their hands on that patented Ives reverse sequencer—they divvied up rolling stock and motive power to add to their lines.

But American Flyer wasn't through with its introductions for 1928. Ogden Coleman's designers must have been a pretty smug group as the most fabulous toy train ever built rolled down the main line under wide-eyed dealers' noses. The Mayflower was similar to the President's Special, but it had been electroplated with cadmium plating and buffed to a mirror shine. Four gleaming passenger cars hung off its drawbar, creating a silvery train more than six feet (1.8m) long that could suck all the wind out of a kid's lungs on Christmas morning.

As the calendar clicked over to 1929, American Flyer, Lionel, and Dorfan were riding high as the stock market soared, buy-now-pay-later plans were sweeping the country, bootleg booze was flowing freely despite Prohibition, and everyone was singing, "We're in the money."

Almost unnoticed, a former sergeant in the Great War who became a toy salesman had become a millionaire by 1925. He had also dis-covered toy trains. Named Louis Marx, he had made a fortune selling mechan-ical tin toys, such as the Alabama Minstrel Dancer and Zippo the Climbing Monkey. In 1927, Marx bought the dies for his Joy Line trains from the Girard Model Works in Girard, Pennsylvania. These were cheap, tin, wind-up trains, more of a threat to William Hafner, who was still making wind-ups, than to the big three. But Louis Marx had a gift for extracting profits through volume sales that would make all his competitors squirm later on.

Taking advantage of Ives' demise, American Flyer lifted the Ives Model 1134 steam locomotive boiler and cab casting, and made it AF's No. 4692 Atlantic-type steamer. Dropping this casting onto its own motor, drive train, and couplers, and adding the Ives tender casting to its trucks created a quick fix that ran in the Flyer catalog for two years. Dorfan also borrowed the castings, while Lionel used the 1134's tender for years.

When Ives went belly-up in 1929, many of its accessories that both Lionel and American Flyer had been buying to relabel for their own lines became available without the price tag. This ubiquitous Ives two-door station wore both Lionel and American Flyer signage from 1928–1938.

One advantage of the 1134's design was that it cut away the catwalk on the loco's right side in order to get at motor brushes and to facilitate oiling. This easy-maintenance feature became standard on all future American Flyer steam locos of the prewar period.

All the other Wide gauge sets remained in the American Flyer line through 1929, while lower-cost sets were added, such as the Lone Scout passenger set, hauled by a shortened, trim-stripped version of the Shasta loco, the No. 4635 electric. The 4686 Flying Colonel was also a slightly stripped-down version of the President's Special, which sold for one dollar less.

The 1920s had been a decade of practically exponential growth for American Flyer. The line had grown from local sales in Chicago to become a national product line, giving longer-established industry leaders strong competition. American Flyer was reaching for the market share brass ring with its 1928 offerings when, suddenly, the carousel ground to a screeching halt.

Stock market investors who had fueled the soaring numbers now watched their life savings disappear in the black hole of margin calls, as stock prices tumbled. Banks that had floated those buy-now-pay-later schemes began closing their doors. "Pay Later" became "Pay Now." Across the country, brokers in financial houses tried to fly away from their problems through their office windows high above the streets. People of wealth and property reached into their once-deep pockets and found only lint.

The toy train manufacturers collectively took a deep breath and surveyed their options. Ogden Coleman was a canny businessman, hedging his bets with many investments in other companies. But as corporate doors closed and unemployed workers spilled into the streets, even he must have felt the cold chill of failure.

Top: A three-piece all-red 3211 caboose waits on a siding. This 1935 O gauge American Flyer model sits on Type 8 trucks with odd brass journals. Note the porthole rear windows.

Left Bottom: Between 1921 and 1929, American Flyer added a more prototypical look to its freight car fleet with six-and-a-half-inch (16.5cm), eight-wheel cars. This Model 1118 tank car is typical of the line, showing many hand-added components such as tank straps and handrails.

Right Bottom: American Flyer launched its Hummer line of low-cost wind-up train sets in 1915. These pretty little passenger cars arrived in the 1930s, competing with Louis Marx's Joy Line trains for the bottom rung of the marketplace.

CHAPTER THREE

DERAILED BY THE GREAT DEPRESSION

All the toy train manufacturers—with the singular exception of Louis Marx and his very low-priced toys—were in the same sinking boat. Just as the bottom fell out of absolutely everything, they were peddling their most expensive Standard gauge and Wide gauge train sets. These big trains were aimed at rich people with disposable income to indulge their little heirs and heiresses. Now, that income was being used to buy day-old bread and dried beans. Although the American economy was circling the bowl, some of the most beautiful toy trains ever designed came out of American Flyer, Lionel, and Dorfan shops during the 1930s. Both Lionel and American Flyer, each seeking to expand its market, resurrected their steam locomotives in 1930.

To save on labor costs, Lionel had shifted design and toolmaking offshore to Italy in the mid-1920s. With the hearty support of the ravaged postwar Italian government, Lionel built the *Società Meccanica la Precisa* in Naples. As Lionel shifted to steam production, the creations that rolled forth from the Naples shop were stamped-steel toys resembling no known (or at least very obscure) prototypes. Each steam engine was draped with copper or nickel piping; wheel spokes and cowcatchers were painted bright red. They looked, well, Italian. But they were elegant, and real locomotive engineers were paid to praise the models in ads and on the catalog covers.

"Just like mine," said New York Central engineer Bob Butterworth, holding a Lionel Standard gauge 400E, a 4-4-4 stamped-steel loco that looked nothing like his big 4-6-4 J-3

Hudson. However toylike these gaudy baubles appeared, they ran well and began filling Lionel's Standard gauge and O gauge lines.

During 1930 and 1931, steam sets held the spotlight for American Flyer as well. Americans were looking over their shoulders as the Great Depression took hold. Banks ran out of money. The jobless lined up outside soup kitchens. Ogden returned to steamer production in Flyer's O gauge line as well as introducing two new Wide gauge steam engines, the 4672 and the 4683, each with its own passenger cars.

One can only imagine that a sort of blind optimism flourished in the administrative offices where Ogden Coleman, Joshua Lionel Cowen, and the Forchheimer brothers directed their production and sales efforts. These owners of American Flyer, Lionel, and Dorfan, respectively, were convinced that there were still enough customers untouched by the harsh economic reality who would buy the big trains. Perhaps they believed the message of newly elected President Franklin Roosevelt—"We have nothing to fear but fear itself"—conveyed in his 1932 inauguration speech. All these owners of toy train companies had been raised in upper middle-class comfort, where money was always just, well, there. They seemed to be caught up in the competition among themselves as opposed to the reality of lowered sales numbers and slipping profits. They didn't stop searching for new customers, as they continued to pour expensive resources into their most narrow market niche.

Designs for the American Flyer O gauge locos didn't fare as well as those for the Wide gauge steamers. The Model 3192 of 1930 was a cast-iron throw-back affair to the days of 1919 and the Model 1225, but the 3192 was trimmed with brass nameplates, orange drive wheels with nickel rims, and add-on handrails. A square was cut out of the side of the engine to allow access to the motor brushes, and the motor inside had no reversing mechanism. It was a dowdy old hen that only ran in one direction and pulled a modest little four-wheel tender. It was obvious that American Flyer was playing catch-up again.

By 1931, American Flyer was tinkering with boiler castings, adding pilot and trailing trucks to its locos. A quick look over the fence at Lionel showed the Flyer designers that

the interest in jumped-up, key-wind engines, stuffed with electric motors, had evaporated; AF's new steamers needed a facelift to compete. The Model 3302 loco filled the vacuum.

This engine was a beauty, featuring brass piping, handrails, and flag holders on the pilot deck. A red "fire" glowed in the fire box, while actual side rods churned away at the drivers. Riding behind the locomotive was a facsimile of a Vanderbilt tender above a pair of four-wheel trucks. The smokestack, bell, and steam dome were brass turnings fit into the No. 6 boiler/cab one-piece casting. The headlight in the center of the smoke box was shaded by a stamped-tin visor.

Most interesting was the use of American Flyer's electro-mechanical reverse system, which allowed remote-control reversing—at least most of the time. The remote system could be locked out with a lever and manually reversed by using a small handle in the cab. This lock-out feature was adopted throughout the Flyer toy train line, which speaks volumes about its engineers' confidence in the remote-control reverse design, or it might simply have been an answer to the high number of customer complaints. The manual reverse lever was common to both Lionel and American Flyer, even showing up in postwar models.

By 1932, the fragile cast side rods had been replaced by nickel-plated steel rods on the Model 3326. Larger drivers, a muzzlelike encasement that completely encircled the headlight, and a deeper fire box gave this loco a brutish look, like a mobile artillery piece.

The next three years saw a continuing shift toward cost cutting in the steam engine line: the single die-cast boiler was replaced by split casting, as used in the 3316 2-4-2 locomotive of 1932. The Vanderbilt tender also lost its graceful side molding, which separated the coal box from the rounded water tank. The new tender was slab-sided. Flyer's die-cast tenders gave way to sheet-metal designs that eventually lost all their character, becoming simple boxes on wheels—and often reverting from eight wheels in prototypical four-wheel trucks to become toylike four-wheelers.

In 1934, American Flyer shifted from die-cast boilers to lower-cost, sheet-metal designs, such as the Model 617 that sold for four dollars. These stamped-steel locomotives

THE NAME GAME

The earliest toy trains, pulled by string, powered by live steam, or propelled along the carpet by a spring motor, usually used real railroad names on their locomotives and cars. The Baltimore & Ohio; the New York, New Haven & Hartford; the New York Central; and the Pennsylvania Railroad trains clicked and clattered around their track ovals in American homes. As the competition for shelf space heated up after World War I and into the Great Depression, realistic touches, such as railroad heralds on rolling stock and locomotive tenders, gave way to the toy manufacturers' names. They were rubber-stamped and framed in brass plaques: Lionel Lines, American Flyer Lines, Ives Electric Trains, and Dorfan Lines. Sometimes, both a railroad herald and the toy company name appeared.

The advertising value of seeing the manufacturer's name on the loco or car outweighed any concerns about verisimilitude when it came to pushing product. Lionel pursued realism in its die-castings and, eventually, in its use of real railroad names, especially after World War II. Kids wanted to play with the trains they saw pounding across railroad intersections; even if the cars were not quite up to scale, having a real name stamped on their sides let the imagination do the rest.

Curiously, American Flyer decided to stay with the "American Flyer Lines" name, even after the business was bought up by A.C. Gilbert in 1937. While prototypical paint schemes were used on passenger cars and locomotives, more often than not, the steam loco trailed an "American Flyer Lines" tender and the passenger diesel was named Comet or Flash.

Today, it's often hard to find the manufacturer's name on a ten-pound, prototypically perfect, scale-model electric locomotive. Real railroad names are the norm on today's motive power and rolling stock. Only collectors cherish those big Lionel "L" logos and shiny brass American Flyer heralds decorating many very expensive prewar train sets.

RIGHT: Two little Hummers, a 515 coach and the 513 observation car, bring up the tail end of a charming passenger train. The Hummer line was launched by American Flyer in the 1930s to compete in the really cheap toy train market dominated by Louis Marx. Note the manufacturer's name proudly announcing the lineage of the cars.

continued as part of the AF line into the late 1930s, like shiny black mile markers along American Flyer's downhill path.

During this period, Lionel was going in the opposite direction in its designs and engineering. Lionel designers had championed sheet-metal locomotives from the start, building dazzling creations such as the Model 400E in Standard gauge and the 260E in O gauge. These were elegant, graceful designs, tarted up with the copper, nickel, and red trim from the artisans in the Italian shops. Lionel eased into die-casting, but its approach favored prototypical realism that came to fruition in the 1937 scale model 700E J-3 Hudson.

The die-casting champs in the 1920s and early 1930s were the Forchheimer brothers, who owned Dorfan. The Dorfan Alloy castings, which came out of the company's Newark, New Jersey, shop, gave Dorfan an immediate price-durability edge over Lionel and also challenged American Flyer. The naturally "slick" castings required no lubrication for axles and shafts that passed through holes in the metal. They offered their locomotives in kits to be assembled as "educational" toys. And Dorfan motors were strong, which helped the company carve out a significant chunk of shelf space during the holidays.

Meanwhile, both American Flyer and Dorfan stayed with a toylike look in their trains and their castings, which, while durable and cost-efficient, still possessed the cast-iron crudeness of pre–World War I models. As technology permitted, Lionel moved steadily toward a more prototypical look, with its cast-on details, allowing customers to recognize it at a glance and giving American Flyer a run for its money for decades.

Although American Flyer locomotives up to this time had yet to evolve from a toylike appearance, the company's rolling stock was certainly looking more realistic. While passenger cars remained the focus of most Flyer train sets, the freight line had taken a large leap forward in 1924 with the introduction of the 3000 series cars. Previously, Flyer freight cars were nothing more than little four-wheel toys, charming in their lithographed colors and looking cute trailing behind a little wind-up loco, but they were hopelessly outdated compared to freight sets from Lionel and Dorfan. Even the cars that sported prototypical four-wheel trucks—

TOP: Rolling on undersize Type 8 freight trucks, this stamped-steel wrecking crane was a colorful addition to an American Flyer O gauge work train between 1936 and 1938. The oversize hook was manually operated.

TOP: Among the low-end offerings of the wind-up line, this 1933 Model 31 is made of stamped steel and features a battery-operated headlight and some bits of brass trim.

Bottom: A little six-and-a-half-inch (16.5cm), low-priced, box-cab electric, the Model 1093, was a one-year wonder in 1930. It's a clunky loco with an outsized headlight and minimal features which did not include reverse.

OPPOSITE: Rounding a corner at the head end of a passenger consist is a 1930 Model 3105 New Haven–style box-cab locomotive. The little four-wheeler was made of stamped steel with rugged detail work for heavy play.

the six-and-one-half-inch (16.5cm) 1100 series cars—were squeezed and flattened, looking like little kids wearing their dads' big shoes.

Flyer's nine-and-one-half-inch (24cm) freight cars in the early 3000 series, which ran from 1924 to 1927, stretched out into more prototypical dimensions. A number of railroad heralds and paint schemes were lithographed on their stamped-steel sides, courtesy of Ogden Coleman's lithography company.

As they appeared in the American Flyer catalogs between 1924 and 1926, they even had air tanks suspended below their frames as a nod to underbody detail. Sadly, this was not the case on the real toy cars; by 1927 the tanks had magically disappeared from print, courtesy of an artist's airbrush. Buying from American Flyer catalogs was always a chancy proposition, since designers had a compulsion to tinker with details, promising new "features" that never materialized and dropping lines with no advance notice. An American Flyer catalog was no more than a "guide" to the product line until the company went out of business in 1966.

These freight cars marked the high-water line of American Flyer's lithographic decoration. In 1928, the 3200 series cars emerged spray-painted with colorful enamel, but minus the railroad heralds and rows of black rivets. If the 3200 freight cars lack "railroady" paint-scheme touches, they did look much better than their predecessors. The 3000 cars' pair of four-wheel trucks were too close together, creating a pronounced overhang that kept the 1924 models looking like they were balancing on a teeter-totter. The trucks on the 3200 series were closer to the end of the cars, giving the cars a more prototypical appearance.

From 1920 to the 1930s, Flyer passenger cars also reflected the company's changing fortunes. The rolling stock ranged from little four-wheel toys that chased the early cast-iron locos around track ovals, to a series of Illini and Columbia passenger sets offering cars nine and one-half inches (24cm) long that had air tanks, many windows, and opening doors. The Model 3000 Illini mail car even had a mailbag pick-up arm. A shorter eight-and-one-quarter-inch (21cm) series was offered in 1928. Finally, this move to scale proportions ended with a set—the 3380 series—that featured

Top: A fine, mid-size, O gauge steam engine for freight or passenger service, the Model 3310-3316 locomotive built on a Type 8 boiler was all stamped steel trimmed in brass and made its appearance in the early 1930s. The lever protruding behind the smokestack on this 3315/16 engine is the manual reverse lever, used when the remote reverse is locked out.

Bottom: The Model 421 steel crossing gate added some realism to American Flyer O gauge layouts in the 1930s. This gate is a transition piece made following the dissection of Ives by Lionel and American Flyer in 1929. It has an Ives base, a Lionel gate, and a shanty built by American Flyer. The accessory was sold in a Lionel box with an American Flyer number on it.

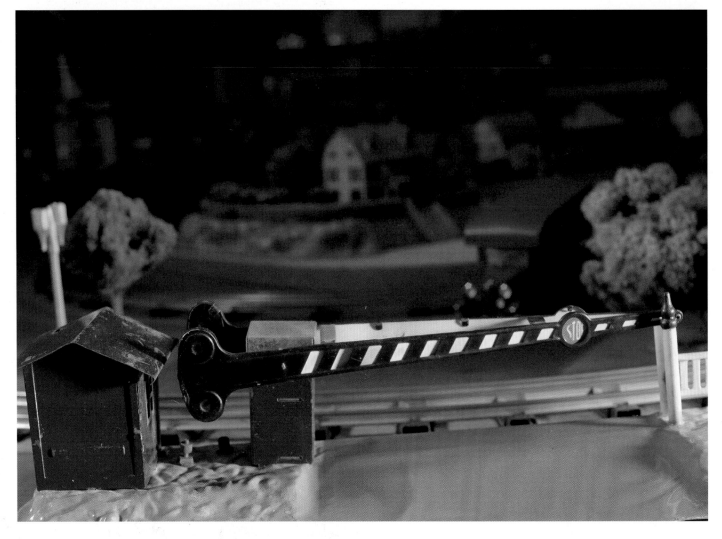

cars eleven inches (28cm) long with celluloid windows and cast-iron air tanks, spot-welded together for durability. You had a choice of one color: "Victory Red." The roofs were sprayed a slightly darker shade of red than the bright red sides. These Ambassador cars more closely resembled their prototypes and stayed in the line until 1935.

Tight radius curves dictated by the O gauge, three-rail track also shaped cars and locos alike. American Flyer launched a "compressed" series of 1930s passenger cars to trail behind their lower-cost locos: the six-and-one-half-inch (16.5cm) "Wide-Low Profile" cars, and the eight-and-one-quarter-inch (21cm) passenger cars.

The six-and-one-half-inch (16.5cm) cars suffered from the same "little car over enormous four-wheel trucks" look that dogged the shorter freight cars. They were only a short jump up from the tiny four-wheelers of the teens and '20s. "American Flyer Lines" was rubber-stamped above the line of four windows and below the stampings was printed either the car serial number, or "A.F.L."

American Flyer's eight-and-one-quarter-inch (21cm) cars were stretched out to six windows in length and looked better over their rigid-frame trucks. The "American Flyer Lines" tags were decaled over the enamel paint jobs. A nice non sequitur in this series was the 3179 observation car of 1935. It was cadmium-plated to a silvery luster.

Over on the East Coast, Dorfan passenger cars featured die-cast passengers' heads and shoulders fastened in place behind the window sills as well as handrails and other added features. Lionel passenger cars, meanwhile, were truly elegant, including the giant State sets in Standard gauge that were fully detailed inside. The O gauge cars were not far behind, excellent in both concept and finish, and sold for correspondingly higher prices.

The exception to Lionel's pricey rolling stock was the set created for the 1930 "Winner" train set, which consisted of a steam loco, four freight cars, track, and a transformer for $3.95. The set was built ostensibly by the "Winner Toy Company" to keep it at arm's length from sullying the Lionel name. By 1934, the "Lionel Jr." set took advantage of old Ives stock to trail three passenger cars behind a steam loco. However, even the quality of Dorfan's and Lionel's cheapest

SPRUNG SPRING CAUSES CHRISTMAS CHAOS

Cost-cutting procedures were instituted at every turn of the engineering process during the Depression. As a result, production problems plagued the manufacturing shop. Despite the lean times, wind-up locomotives were still a hot item during the country's financial pinch. Each steel spring that was used to propel a wind-up loco was about eight feet long (2.4m). The last four inches (10cm) of the spring were annealed so it wouldn't break after being wound over and over again. Engineers tried a cost-cutting method in the annealing process. Each locomotive was wound up and run before shipping and every engine passed the test. But the new spring broke after two or three windings. Returning the busted locomotive to American Flyer required a thirty-five-cent handling fee, but as the first thousand broken locos began arriving the day after Christmas, no one cared if the thirty-five cents was included or not. Thousands more began to flow through the service department and soon the Halsted Street plant was awash in snapped springs and letters of complaint. Estimates put the number of wind-up American Flyer locomotives shipped to dealers with defective springs at about one million units.

This odd little lithographed trolley was added to the line in 1933 as a single powered unit. It had a huge front light and no reverse. No wind-up gremlins plagued this little electric.

HAPPY DAYS AT HADHISWAY HALL

When Ogden Coleman moved from his mother's house in River Forest in 1929 and built a new house at 120 Meadow Lane in Winnetka, Illinois, his sisters, Margaret and Julia, named it "Hadhisway Hall," claims his daughter, Kirby Coleman Brown, "because it was the only time he had his way. He wanted a colonial house worthy of his Southern wife, whose grandfather, Edmund Kirby Smith, was the last Civil War general to surrender. Daddy was an adoring husband and a fun father."

Interviewed by the authors in March 2002, Kirby shared memories of the busy, happy days she spent with her mother, father, and three brothers at Hadhisway Hall. Although Ogden was a hard-working man, Kirby remembers her father as adventuresome and always ready to have a good time: "Daddy used to leave early and come home late. When I was little—and I hate to admit this—I asked my mother, 'Who was that nice man with the Juicy Fruit gum?'

"In the winter, he'd tie our sleds behind his car and drive us around the driveway. We always had games going on. There was table tennis and a pool table in the basement, and we had a full-size tennis court in the backyard of the two-acre property. I guess we were very fortunate in those days.

"The whole top floor at 120 Meadow Lane was left open for the trains. My two older brothers had the big trains laid out and I had the Narrow gauge [O gauge]. Johnny, the youngest, claimed the HO and had it on a table. But we all played with all of them. At Christmas we always had a train running around the tree. Because Daddy was president of the Toy Manufacturers Association for a period of time, often experimental toys were sent to us to be tested. I remember the Rhythm Bike. You bounced up and down on it to make it go. It didn't survive. We broke it in half." Ogden called his kids his "Testing Society."

Top: This architectural rending of Hadhisway Hall depicts the only time "Oggie" Coleman had his way when it came to domestic issues.
Bottom: In 1898 Ogden Coleman was just six years old. This scion to Will Coleman's fortune would one day have his own baronial hall.

sets rivaled the best American Flyer could send to dealers as the Great Depression's grip tightened.

By the end of 1932, over at the Halsted Street plant in Chicago, everything started to collapse. Sales figures for the Wide gauge trains were dismal—the big trains simply were not selling. The number of sets offered for sale dropped from eighteen to eleven. The era of the "Rich Boy's Gauge" was coming to an end. There would be some tinkering with the sets languishing in inventory and a few "new" sets were produced through 1934, but by 1933, Ogden Coleman had discontinued production of the line. What could be sold was kept in the catalog until 1937, but the twelve-year experiment with Wide gauge as a revenue generator came to an end much earlier than that.

Of all the Wide gauge trains designed, the saddest end came to the most prestigious President's Special sets. The beautiful two-tone blue model with brass trimming had sold—or rather not sold—for $100. When the Special was cadmium-plated to a silvery sheen and renamed The Mayflower, the price went up to $150. While these gleaming sets were used as crowd stoppers in show windows at Marshall Fields in Chicago and John Wanamaker's department store in Philadelphia, very few customers were willing to part with that much cash. The boxed Mayflower sets gathered dust in storage, thirty boxes to a skid, for a few years until the company was taken over by A.C. Gilbert in 1937.

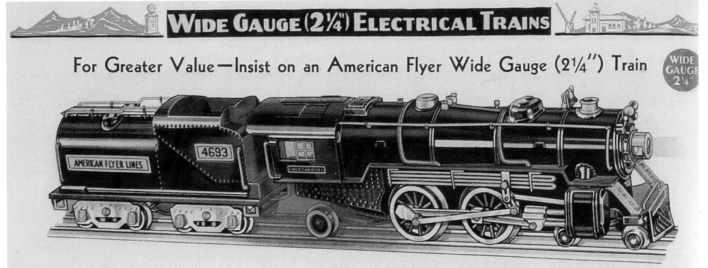

TOP: A vast layering of brass dolls up this 1934 Wide gauge 4694 steam locomotive as it rolls into oblivion. By 1934, Wide gauge sales were in the pits and no amount of added doodads would rescue the line.
BOTTOM: The Model 4693 engine-tender combination hauled the Century passenger set in 1932. Although Wide gauge steamers are touted as a "greater value" in this ad, Wide gauge trains were not popular and were discontinued in 1933.

OPPOSITE: In 1930, American Flyer brought out its "Wide/Low Profile" passenger cars. The Model 3152 observation car is one of the eight-wheel, six-and-a-half-inch (16.5cm) cars. This wide, stubby car is trimmed in brass at the windows, doors, and journal boxes. The observation deck and railing are brass colored, and the hanging awning fringe looks like the upper jaw of a meat eater.

TOP: Trailing behind the 1934 Wide gauge 4694 would be this equally gaudy Vanderbilt-type tender complete with red sideboards, brass handrails, and gray trucks with brass journals. The beautiful tender would loyally follow its locomotive straight into the scrap yard by the end of the year.

BOTTOM: An O gauge tank car circa the 1930s rests on Type 8 freight trucks with brass journals. The tank mounts are brass colored as are the tank straps and dome—but that's why they're called "toy" trains. It's a charming interpretation that looks great flashing down the main line.

AMERICAN

FLYER

57

TOP: Maury Romer worked for W.O. Coleman Jr. and A.C. Gilbert in a variety of positions. His experiences in both companies with the people who built and sold Flyer trains has lent us great insight into each company's operational idiosyncrasies.
OPPOSITE: The 4694 helped lead the steam engine roll-out into the Wide gauge line in 1929. This fourteen-and-a-half-inch (37cm)-long loco-motive has remote-control reverse and not much else. It seemed to be incomplete, rushed out the door to fill a gap in the line. On the original, there are no crossheads at the pistons to support the drive rods and the brass builder's plaque is blank. This 1932 model has a crosshead and triangular valve gear and a more prototypical look. The casting origi-nally belonged to Ives.

A telephone call came in one day and the two remaining skids of Mayflower trains were transferred to the service department. The boxes were opened and a short disassembly line was created. One man opened the boxes, another removed the locomotives' reusable motors, and two other men took turns with a heavy lead hammer smashing the plated engines and cars into pieces, then tossing what remained into the scrap box. A few sets were saved by employees who wanted them, but, for the most part, the most famous trains in American Flyer's Wide gauge fleet were hammered into junk.

Maury Romer, who supervised the sad demolition, remembered years later, "I decided I'd like one also . . . and one additional locomotive and two extra cars. . . . We decid-ed to move with the plant to New Haven [the A.C. Gilbert plant in Connecticut]. The box of trains came along with us. We kept them in a closet off our front room for some time. Mrs. Romer used to ask me, 'When are you ever going to get rid of that heavy box? Every time I clean that closet I have to move that box.' I sold the whole lot for $100."

By 1935, all was dissolution and dyspepsia at American Flyer. No one wanted the company's Wide gauge electric trains. The O gauge line was respectable, but nothing to shout about, and Louis Marx's Joy Line trains were killing Flyer in the low-cost, high-volume market. If that wasn't bad enough, labor unrest was seething on the sixth floor.

The Depression had frozen or reduced workers' salaries. As communists agitated for labor reforms, corporations found themselves harried by union organizers. The United Paper, Novelty, and Toymakers Union was pounding on Lionel's door and would eventually organize Joshua Lionel Cowen's paternalistic fiefdom in 1937. Of course, Lionel could fall back on its design shops at the *Società Meccanica la Precisa* in Naples. But even there, the Italian government was growing wildly unstable.

The big rage in labor protest was the sit-down strike. Instead of leaving the factory and marching around with picket signs, the workers just sat down at their stations and refused to leave until their grievances had been heard and—ostensibly—met. American Flyer's turn came in 1935, when sly tiptoeing around and whispered meetings resulted in the

Locomotive Assembly Division on the sixth floor sitting down and refusing to work. The dissension quickly spread to the Car Assembly and Accessory sections.

The executives were flabbergasted that such a thing could happen at American Flyer, and company bigwigs raced around pointing fingers, speaking loudly, and trying to intim-idate workers into abandoning their strike. Finally, clearer heads prevailed. A spokesman, Al Lyche, head of service cor-respondence, was sent to talk to the strikers, or rather sitters. After a while, everyone was laughing and the tension relaxed. Families were allowed to visit the sitters, who lowered pails from the sixth-floor windows to get fresh food and see their kids. Three or four days later, the strike petered out without great effect.

The only bittersweet sunshine to illuminate American Flyer's rather drab days was the failure of Dorfan in 1934. Milton and Julius Forchheimer had built Dorfan into a major player in the toy train industry during the late 1920s. Their die-cast locomotives, line of rolling stock, and accessories had challenged Lionel to shear away from stamped-steel motive power toward die-casting. Lionel had also resurrected its own "Bild-A-Loco" train kits of 1919 to counter Dorfan's popular "Loco-Builder" sets.

Unfortunately, the zinc-copper compound patented under the name "Dorfan Alloy" that had propelled Dorfan into a strong competitive position proved to be inherently flawed. Locomotives began pouring back into Dorfan with cracked shells or with shells so distorted that turning shafts were pinched to immobility. The alloy was not stable. As it aged, it began to crack and soften. Besides the crumbling locomotives, the great amount of hand labor required to assemble Dorfan's exquisite rolling stock—a passenger car often contained as many as 117 parts—was sucking up the profits before they reached the bottom line. In 1934, after a ten-year run, the Forchheimer brothers closed the doors of the Newark, New Jersey, plant. It is rare today to find a Dorfan locomotive that is not spider-webbed with fine cracks and fissures.

Another bit of good news for American Flyer was that Lionel was now in receivership, as hard-eyed bankers reviewed every one of Cowen's executive decisions. The clash

American Flyer built a number of streamlined locomotives matching popular prototypes of the mid- to late 1930s. The M-10000 was Union Pacific's answer to reviving travel by rail and "making it an event," according to UP advertising and public relations. This M-10000 model arrived in 1936 with the power car, two coaches, and an observation car. The set was modified and kept in the line until 1939.

AMERICAN

FLYER

Locomotives and rolling stock, purchased in quantity following the war, were now rusting away on sidings. Corporate executives and entrepreneurs were all looking for a way to jump-start their own industries.

In the locomotive industry, a simultaneous "Aha!" went up at the offices of the Union Pacific Railroad and the Chicago, Burlington & Quincy Railroad. Those streamlined epiphanies would salvage the fortunes of one toy train maker and postpone the downward slide of another. Even Louis Marx, who never stopped making money, paid attention.

The race to field the first streamlined train was won by Union Pacific, which built its M-10000 streamliner in partnership with the Pullman Car and Manufacturing Company near Chicago. The yellow and brown aluminum train, powered by a "distillate" engine, weighed in at 124 tons (112t). It beat the Zephyr into service by two months, but the Zephyr's diesel-electric engine and welded design held the technological edge.

Lionel had been bird-dogging Union Pacific, creating a publicity partnership to obtain train plans and specifications. These specs were turned into an O gauge, 1/45 scale model, designed to run on new, wider-radius, O-72 track. The receivers peering over Lionel's shoulder approved the new model—along with a little wind-up handcar featuring Mickey and Minnie Mouse that sold for one dollar.

American Flyer designers got the green light from Ogden Coleman to begin creating a model of the CB&Q Zephyr at the same time the Budd Company began construction of the super lightweight, high-speed prototype in 1932. Realizing the importance of the publicity that would be generated by a scale model of the new train, Budd and the CB&Q readily provided the plans.

American Flyer's production solution involved casting the Zephyr in aluminum, using sand molds, while Lionel chose die-casting and sheet steel for its M-10000. Flyer's project manager, Simon Chaplin, had tried using tin-plated steel, but that material got badly scratched during the production process, turning the required shiny appearance into a dull gray. Since Flyer's die-casting vendor explained that the company's die-casting machines were incapable of producing the desired shells, sand molds were the only

of personalities between Joshua Lionel Cowen and Ogden Coleman had come to the surface during the carving up of Ives in 1929. As Ives' moldering assets were divvied up between Lionel and American Flyer, Ogden and Joshua discovered that they didn't like each other. They couldn't even stand to be in the same room together. Ogden had thrown in his lot with Lionel, only to come away with scraps, while Lionel got the lion's share from the joint venture. Lionel funneled the cheap chunks of Ives into low-cost locos and cars (the Winner and Lionel Jr. lines, for example) but, aside from the excellent patented reverse mechanism, Ives' impact on Lionel's bottom line was negligible.

By now, President Franklin Roosevelt had signed the repeal of Prohibition and was thrashing around in an alphabet soup of government work agencies and economic Band-Aids. The railroads themselves had fallen on hard times.

American Flyer rolled out its own model of the Milwaukee Road Hiawatha shrouded steamer in 1935. Like its Lionel 1935 counterpart, the AF Hiawatha featured a die-cast shell and a 4-4-2 Atlantic-type wheel arrangement. Curiously, on the four-wheel leading truck, only the front pair of wheels actually swiveled to follow the track. The second pair was fixed to the engine's frame, and there was only one pair of wheels in the rear four-wheel truck. The entire Hiawatha set plus cars and a forty-inch (101.6cm) loop of track cost $16.50.

remaining solution. Using these molds required considerable grinding. Each train component was cast in two halves and fused together down the roof center lines.

Budd kept changing the train's contours, forcing American Flyer designers to redo their own molds. These molds were changed eight times before the final design was locked down in 1934. As aluminum bodies arrived at the Halsted Street plant, drum grinders with oil-stone surfaces cleaned up the rough center lines, while the final polishing used jeweler's rouge to buff the wheels. Plastic films were affixed over window ports, braces were attached at the floor level, and spring-loaded coupling tabs joined the articulated

AMERICAN

FLYER

THE GOD OF THE WEST WIND BLOWS FAIR

In the fall of 1932, Charles F. Kettering provided the key to building the first complete diesel-electric locomotive in the United States. Kettering was General Motors' vice president of research. Working with metallurgists, his design team developed new alloys that allowed the company to build a lightweight, two-cycle, eight-cylinder diesel engine. What distinguished the engine was its power-to-weight ratio: it was light enough to be mounted on a locomotive frame, yet powerful enough to pull a train at high speed.

A lightweight, high-speed train had already been ordered from the E. G. Budd Manufacturing Company in Philadelphia, Pennsylvania, but it lacked sufficient motive power. A meeting was held in the office of company president Ralph Budd in the spring of 1933 to bring together Budd's revolutionary, aluminum, shot-welded, streamlined train, and the new General Motors diesel engine. An existing 195-mile (314km) route between Kansas City and Omaha was chosen for the train's initial revenue run. As the meeting ended, one of the Budd people mentioned that the train needed a name. The "last word" in trains was suggested as a theme. The last word in the dictionary was "Zymurgy," the practice of fermentation, as in the making of alcoholic beverages. Not a good choice for a streamlined train. At the time, Ralph Budd was reading Chaucer's *Canterbury Tales*. In this collection of stories, renaissance is typified through the actions of the god of the west wind, Zephyrus. Following the meeting, Budd made a phone call to Alfred Cotsworth Jr., who had chaired the previous meeting. When they hung up, the train was called the Chicago, Burlington & Quincy Zephyr.

On June 17, 1933, the CB&Q ordered the 600-horsepower Model 201A diesel engine for Budd's super-lightweight Zephyr train. The locomotive and three cars weighed a total of 169,000 pounds, less than one heavyweight passenger car at the time. The articulated train would be 196 feet (60m) long and cost about $200,000. Its cruising speed would be one hundred miles per hour (161kph), topping out at 120 mph (193kph) on the straightaways. That was as fast as many private airplanes flew at the time.

The Chicago, Burlington & Quincy Zephyr pulled out of the Budd factory on April 7, 1934, and on its trial run reached a speed of 109 miles an hour (68kph). On May 26, 1934, the Zephyr broke all records for a nonstop run from Denver to Chicago, leaving at dawn and arriving at dusk in time to roll onto the World's Fair stage to climax the "Wings of the Century" transportation pageant. As the crowd went crazy, railroad passenger transportation changed forever.

LEFT TOP: A lineup of streamlined locomotives (from the left): a shrouded Pennsylvania Railroad Pacific-type steamer, the Union Pacific City of Denver, the CB&Q Zephyr, and the Milwaukee Road Hiawatha Atlantic-type steam engine—all featured in American Flyer's 1936 catalog. The big news inside, however, was that their semiscale Hudson locomotive beat Lionel to the punch by a year.

RIGHT TOP: Silently whooshing down a cleared main line, the CB&Q Pioneer Zephyr makes its record run from Denver to Chicago. People lined the route to watch the little streamliner dash past at one hundred miles per hour (161kph). In 1935 American Flyer launched its own Zephyr series, adding models as new streamliners were shipped out by the railroads.

OPPOSITE: This is a head-on look at American Flyer's 1935 model of the famous CB&Q Zephyr streamliner. It is wider and longer than previous Flyer Zephyrs due to the automatic reverse unit and motor wedged into the power car. This modification, requiring a new, wider casting, was done because of customer complaints about having to pick up the car to get at the manual reverse lever concealed beneath the old casting.

cars together. After the final polishing, decals were affixed and ornamental skirts attached over each shared wheel truck (just as in the prototype), and the Model 9900 (also the same as the CB&Q Zephyr prototype) American Flyer Zephyr was ready to roll down the main line.

The final version for 1934 had a two-car train and a power car. For some reason, a manual reverse lever was affixed to an impossible position beneath the skirt of the power car. You had to pick up the car to change direction. Customer complaints forced the change to automatic reverse in 1935. This change required yet another casting adjustment, making the power car wider. Another addition in 1935 was the Silver Streak Zephyr, a five-car train set that looked ever-so-graceful sweeping around a wider, forty-inch (102cm) radius track.

Lionel, meanwhile, covered its bases by turning out a Zephyr clone, choosing to model the Flying Yankee, a short-line train operated by the Maine Central Railroad that ran between Portland, Maine, and Boston, Massachusetts. Lionel designers also demonstrated their masterly control of the die-cast process by producing an elegant, shrouded, O gauge steamer modeled on the Milwaukee Road's cream, orange,

and black Hiawatha 4-4-2. Combining die-cast and sheet-metal shrouding also produced the O gauge Commodore Vanderbilt steam locomotive.

While American Flyer was pushing its own shiny and elegant Zephyrs out the door as fast as it could polish those shells, almost unobserved, Lionel gained a critical technological advantage that, years later, would come back to bite American Flyer. In 1935, Lionel patented a realistic-sounding, on-board whistle.

In Chicago, to hedge its bets on the Zephyr, American Flyer built lithographed versions of the train out of sheet metal. Compared to the cast Zephyr price of twelve dollars, the sheet-metal, electric-powered model with lithographed silver-and-black exterior came off the dealer's shelf at just six dollars. To squeeze the streamliner concept even further, American Flyer produced wind-up, sheet-metal versions. All these sheet-metal trains used a thin grade of steel that didn't hold up to hard play. Many severely dented tin Zephyrs ended up in the trash can a short time after purchase. They are very rare today.

American Flyer continued to milk the market for streamliners with sheet-metal versions of the Milwaukee Road Hiawatha, powered by wind-up and electric motors. They didn't appear in any Flyer catalogs, but were shipped directly to dealers.

Since the real railroads were jumping on the streamliner concept, American Flyer saw no reason to stop churning out models as fast as the stamping presses could produce them. The 1935 model of a loosely based rendition of the Illinois Central's Green Diamond was added to the lineup. With its turreted cab, looking like beetle brows over a prominent die-cast snoot, this sheet-metal power car resembled a big, green, bird head. The arch of diesel stacks on its roof just contributed to the loco's avian appearance. The No. 1322-RT train measured forty-six inches (117cm) in length and was powered by an electric motor with a manual reverse. All of its cars were fully illuminated.

American Flyer's Zephyr

Built in Collaboration With the C.B.&Q.-R.R.

HIGH SPEED STREAMLINE TRAIN

American Flyer's Zephyr

THE LATEST IN STREAMLINE TRAINS

AMERICAN

FLYER

A pair of lithographed, sheet-metal, steam-type streamliners were also produced in 1935. The Model 960T New York Central train set used the same shared-truck articulation as the original Zephyr, but behind a shrouded 0-4-0 steamer with a headlight. The electric, selling for $4.50, and wind-up models, at $1.50, were both built. These cheap, lithographed, little toys did nothing for American Flyer's image in the marketplace.

Lionel had emerged from receivership over the 1934 holidays, based on the sales of its M-10000 streamlined train and impulse sales of its little one dollar Mickey and Minnie Mouse handcar.

By 1936, American Flyer punched out its own Union Pacific M-10005 City of Denver streamliner, made of die-castings and sheet metal, and numbered Model 1730-RW. Stealing a design coup from Lionel, American Flyer built its City of Denver model with conventional trucks under all the cars, which was true to the prototype after which it was named. Lionel continued to build its version as an articulated train.

As the dust settled over the streamliner wars, American Flyer found itself with a lot of unsold streamlined trains. As former American Flyer employee Maury Romer explained, "They were not good-selling items. Generally they were less costly to produce. They were brought out at a time when the railroads seemed to be setting a pattern of streamlining their locos, but you could not get the boys to go for them.

"They were the type of train that Mother or Aunt Bessie would buy for the kid when the menfolks were not around. . . . If you were sitting, relaxed, with your eyes closed, and the word 'locomotive' was mentioned, what was the mental picture that came to you? Almost everyone had a mental picture of a large, steam locomotive with stacks, dome, pilot, cylinders, and loads of active drive rods. No one ever saw a streamliner as a mental picture. And this surely must have had some effect on the sales. Most of our streamliners were flops."

Even on the railroads, streamline shrouds were coming off the steam engines by the late 1930s because of the maintenance nightmares they caused. The little high-speed passenger streamliners had lost their luster. They became short-line footnotes and novelties as highways improved along their routes. The new and brawny E and F Model diesel locomotives from General Motors' Electro-Motive Division hauled freight or passengers and were easily maintained to boot. The M-10000 ended up scrapped during the war and the little Pioneer Zephyr finished its days as an indoor exhibit at Chicago's Museum of Science and Industry.

American Flyer still had one last hurrah up its sleeve, a chance to shore up the company's image and challenge Lionel's realistic die-cast products. Flyer's designers and engineers came up with a model out of the blue, the 1681 Hudson. This locomotive, cataloged in 1936, went way beyond the little 0-4-0 teakettles and dumpy sheet-metal engines that had gone before it.

First of all, it was the first American Flyer, six-driver steam loco. The new Type 12 boiler was a one-piece casting, larger than anything produced by Flyer at that time. It had a remote-control whistle housed in the tender that was triggered when a pick-up passed over the fourth rail in a special section of track. To top Lionel, the locomotive was the most realistically proportioned, modern, O gauge steam engine ever built. The side rods and crosshead action looked great in motion, and traction was aided by the addition of three weights in the cab—two in the floor, looking like a pair of coffins for the crew, and one fastened to the underside of the cab roof. The sheet-metal tender even had a weight affixed to its front above the coaling step.

The 1681 Hudson had a couple of anomalies. First of all, it was a 2-6-4, whereas the prototype Hudson was a 4-6-4. In addition, the 1681 trailing four-wheel truck only contained one axle and two wheels—one pair of journal boxes was empty. The tender was a dreadful tin box with little character. In 1937, that tender was replaced with a cast-aluminum model that was prototypically excellent, complementing the big Hudson. That same year, the trailing truck also received its two remaining wheels. There was joy on the seventh floor when the big Hudson and its new tender headed for the annual New York Toy Fair—the yearly coming-out party for new toy designs.

At the 1937 fair, Lionel arrived with a previously unannounced model, startling the toy train marketplace by

AMERICAN

FLYER

AMERICAN

FLYER

introducing the 700E 4-6-4 J3 Hudson as an exact scale model. It rode on special T-rail track and cost seventy-five dollars. It was a marvel of die-casting art. A special centrifugal casting process had reproduced every detail of the prototype to within three rivets' accuracy. The 700E was Lionel's answer to the 1936 Model 1681 Hudson, produced by American Flyer, and a proclamation to the industry that Lionel was still the toy train industry leader.

Over in Italy, Mussolini's Black Shirt fascist government was nationalizing Italian industry to build armaments, forcing Lionel's Italian connection in Naples to close its doors. By then, the grip of the Depression was easing a bit, and Lionel was slimming down its product line. The big Standard gauge trains were gone and a move toward die-cast realism, in an attempt to reach the hobby market, was fueling Lionel's gradual comeback.

Without a counterpunch to Lionel's scale Hudson, by 1937 American Flyer was tapped out. Its niche in the wind-up train market was under attack by Louis Marx. The streamliner craze had run its course after a brief sprint of success. Wide gauge trains were gone, smashed and scrapped. Even Flyer's O gauge line looked cheap and dowdy next to the elegant steamers available at even the lowest end of Lionel's product line.

"American Flyer is what Dads bought their kids on Christmas Eve when the stores were sold out of Lionel," said one veteran dealer. "Those dads had a selling job to do on Christmas morning."

Though Ogden Coleman, like his father Will, had many business interests other than toy manufacturing, electric trains were more than just another business investment. Ogden transformed the third-floor attic in his home, Hadhisway Hall, to a train space, partitioning it with Celotex panels so holes could be easily cut to allow toy trains to pass through from room to room.

In an interview in 1999 by Bruce D. Manson, Randolph Coleman, Ogden's son, remembered, "In the main part of the house we had Wide gauge. My brother [William Ogden III] had the passenger set —the blue President's Special—and I had the freight. My sister [Kirby] had O gauge trains. . . . When my younger brother [John] became interested in trains, Dad bought him German HO Marklin trains [1935 and 1936]. My father was thinking ahead, and at that time the idea of model trains being realistic was coming in. He began to buy some of the Marklin trains to think about. Should American Flyer go into this fine detail HO?"

With American Flyer limping along, peddling low-cost, stamped sheet-metal steam locos and rolling stock, Coleman was still unwilling to close the company's doors and lay off loyal employees who had been with him for years. Instead, he wanted a buyer, someone who might turn Flyer's fortunes around. One man came to mind. That man was an energetic, resourceful, businessman, who had succeeded at virtually every enterprise he had attempted. But his shrewd buisiness accumen was the very thing that worked against his taking over a foundering, one-product toy company in unstable financial times.

In the fall of 1937, Coleman was invited to A.C. Gilbert's Paradise Game Farm for some upland bird shooting. After walking the trails and blazing away at rising pheasants, the two manufacturers retired to Gilbert's lodge for drinks in front of the large fireplace.

At the last meeting of the Toy Manufacturers of the U.S.A. Gilbert had jokingly ribbed Coleman that the A.C. Gilbert Company planned to bring out a line of HO gauge trains to become a competitor. Coleman suggested that HO gauge was too small for children's play and then added, "Why don't you take over American Flyer?"

Gilbert replied, "Can't afford it."

Now, in front of the crackling fire, Coleman made his pitch. American Flyer's business was no longer profitable and earnings had slipped to a million dollars a year. Gilbert's manufacturing plant in New Haven had the capacity for larger production runs, and the design know-how to make something of the ailing toy line. Coleman's asking price was $600,000. Gilbert listened, but he had not built his business on rash decisions.

The A.C. Gilbert Company was a publicly traded corporation and, in 1936, had just returned $184,195 in dividends to its preferred and common stock holders. In its 1936 annual report, the company showed a net profit of $155,720 against a 1935 profit of $87,443. A.C. Gilbert was rising from the ashes

of the Great Depression that had beaten it down to a loss of $22,078 in 1933. Finding financing for and taking over an unprofitable toy train company seemed a long shot at best. At this juncture, Gilbert turned Coleman down.

Sitting beside Gilbert in the car on the way back to the train station, Coleman played his last card. Rather than see American Flyer shut down, busted up, and sold off, he put together a deal that allowed A.C. Gilbert to take over the company without paying a dime up front. A 5 percent royalty was added to everything Gilbert produced under the American Flyer name, to be paid to the Coleman family who owned all the stock shares. This agreement would continue for twelve years. Coleman was to remain in touch with the business as a consultant, whether Gilbert chose to keep the plant in Chicago or move it to his New Haven manufacturing center.

Gilbert braked to a stop, turned the car around, and headed back to the lodge. A few minutes after arriving, he was on the phone to other Gilbert associates. A deal was in the making.

OPPOSITE BOTTOM: As profits eluded American Flyer in 1936, their dealer price list pushed a line of products. Trains, toy cash registers, toy typewriters, and Structo toys were all peddled to bring in revenue.
BOTTOM: Wide gauge freight cars were spray-painted a variety of colors at the Halsted Street factory and then sent to the assembly line for the addition of considerable details, including brake wheels, handrails, tank straps, and ladders. This 4010 tank car was in the line from 1928 to 1936. The lemon-yellow color, sadly, reflected the fate of the big train market during strapped financial times.

CHAPTER FOUR

A.C. GILBERT TAKES THE THROTTLE

American Flyer had lived in its Halsted Street plant in Chicago since before World War I and had grown to become the second-largest manufacturer of toy trains in the United States. Over time, Ogden Coleman and his associates had watched other companies fade away. Carlisle & Finch chose to quit making toy trains in 1916 to pursue more profitable government work building searchlights and navigation equipment. The legendary Ives Manufacturing Corporation had drowned in red ink, done in by bad business decisions and worse bookkeeping. Dorfan had built its trains too well and pioneered die-casting with an alloy that had betrayed the company. The Forchheimer brothers' New Jersey plant was shuttered as a result. American Flyer itself would not have been a contender in the toy train business had not William Hafner asked the company to take over building his wind-up trains. Curiously, Hafner was still out there, dueling Louis Marx for the bottom rung of the toy train price ladder.

Now, Odgen Coleman had taken a page from Hafner's proposal and offered American Flyer to A.C. Gilbert on a platter, simply for a share of the profits.

Many historians have debated the wisdom of this deal, offering opinions based on Coleman's record as an owner and boss. Former employees have stated that Coleman had largely been an absentee owner, spending too much time checking out his other business interests. Others claim that his managers, who actually ran the company, lacked any vision or risk-taking spirit. They had also let production quality slip. American Flyer had almost always

been playing catch-up to the other manufacturers, spending too much time handling returns and servicing bad workmanship. Still others claim that, near the end, Coleman's health began to decline and his active participation lagged behind the company's needs. Whatever the reasons, American Flyer under the ownership of William Ogden Coleman Jr. had fallen too far behind to regain profitability. By 1937, American Flyer was losing money every time an employee turned on a machine.

Coleman's American Flyer had experienced shining moments: the Wide gauge President's Special and Mayflower locomotives were outstanding examples of the toy maker's art. The 1936 Hudson in O gauge, the first true attempt at a realistic design, had beaten Lionel to the punch by a year. The CB&Q Zephyr O gauge train had been an entrepreneurial case study, however poor its eventual sales. But, in the end, none of these ventures saved American Flyer. That would be the job for A.C. Gilbert.

Gilbert had been approached once before to enter the toy train business. The owner of the Doler Diecast Company had forwarded a letter from one of its customers to Gilbert back in the early 1930s. Milton Forchheimer was looking to get out of the toy train business. Milton and his brother, Julius, owned Dorfan, an American Flyer rival. They were sinking fast in 1932 and sunk by '34. They wanted to unload their tools and dies, enclosing three Dorfan catalogs with the letter. At that time, Gilbert walked away, but the seed had definitely been planted.

With American Flyer's offer agreed to in principle, Gilbert returned to his New Haven plant and gathered together his brother, F.W. Gilbert, who was plant manager, Arthur Adling, the company comptroller, and a few other key buisness associates for a trip to Chicago. They toured the Halsted Street operation and looked over Flyer's financial logs. The company had been run into the ground and was selling its trains based on the lowest possible price in order to clear inventories. A huge infusion of capital, creative design, and advertising were needed to salvage what was left of American Flyer's reputation. However, the toy train line complemented Erector and other Gilbert toys, so the deal was consummated.

Gilbert's first order as new boss was to move the American Flyer Manufacturing Company to his plant in New Haven. The move was eased by the fact that the Halsted Street plant was leased, not owned by Coleman. Still, a new wing had to be built in New Haven to house Gilbert's latest acquisition. All key Flyer employees had the option of coming to Connecticut with the plant, or finding other work in Chicago. Many valuable employees chose to follow the line to New Haven. Their experience eased the slope of Gilbert's learning curve in this new business venture. A service center remained in Chicago to handle repairs on the current line still on dealers' shelves.

As the company's assets and employees were moved to New Haven, planning for American Flyer's new direction had already been influenced by Phil Connell, who had been sales manager in Chicago and kept that job when he moved east. He became aware of the popularity of two-rail track as he examined the growing HO market. The small-scale models, however, were not suited to young children with small hands who needed larger and more rugged toys. On a trip to the Cleveland Model Supply Company in Ohio, Connell was impressed by the company's 3/16-inch (0.48cm) scale, S gauge model trains. Their proportions were more realistic and could be easily adapted to three-rail, O gauge track. After the takeover, Connell presented these views to A.C. Gilbert, and the entrepreneur embraced the realism concept that would give American Flyer a unique and very competitive market position.

While the move to New Haven was taking place during 1938, Gilbert also pursued his original idea of launching a line of HO-scale trains for the hobby market. After being developed in England, the "Half-O" gauge was originally introduced to American hobbyists at the 1933 Century of Progress Fair in Chicago. By the late 1930s John Tyler had created engines and cars from his company, Mantua Metal Products, and Gordon Varney was building HO trains under his name so locomotives and rolling stock were becoming available in the United States.

Gilbert jumped on the small gauge bandwagon with what he called Tru-Model trains—borrowing the name from Erector sets he had made for Sears Roebuck in 1929. The HO

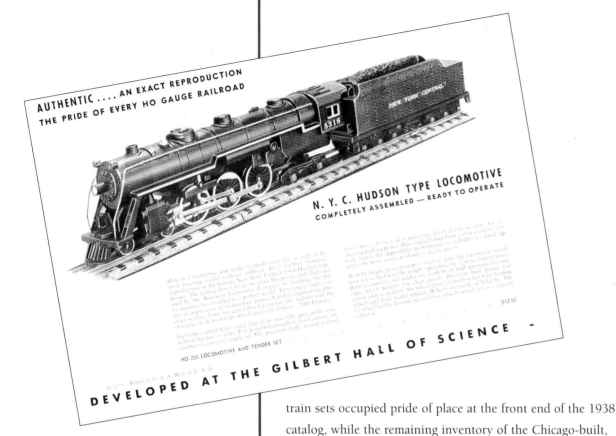

AUTHENTIC.... AN EXACT REPRODUCTION
THE PRIDE OF EVERY HO GAUGE RAILROAD

N. Y. C. HUDSON TYPE LOCOMOTIVE
COMPLETELY ASSEMBLED — READY TO OPERATE

HO-200 LOCOMOTIVE AND TENDER SET

DEVELOPED AT THE GILBERT HALL OF SCIENCE

By 1950s standards, the Gilbert HO gauge Hudson is top of the line in quality. It could be purchased ready-to-run or in kit form and offered not just nail-pulling tractive effort from a 25 to 1 gear ratio, but also gave HO hobbyists real American Flyer smoke and sound effects. Many of these locos are running today and can still haul long, long trains. This model was first offered with Bakelite drivers and metal rims, but was quickly changed over to all-metal wheels.

train sets occupied pride of place at the front end of the 1938 catalog, while the remaining inventory of the Chicago-built, O gauge trains was relegated to the back of the book. Based on a model of the New York Central Hudson, the HO loco-motive's spur gear-drive motor was AC-powered and the engine arrived with Bakelite drive wheels. These were rapidly changed to plastic drivers with brass rims.

American Flyer wasn't the only manufacturer looking to capture the small, scale-model hobby market. Knapp (formerly Knapp Electric and Novelty Company, builders of 2-inch [5.08cm] gauge trains from 1904 to 1913) introduced an oddball E gauge line in ⅛-inch (0.03cm) scale that quickly vanished. Later, Hal P. Joyce came along with his "table-top" or TT gauge at ¹⁄₁₀-inch (0.25cm) scale in 1941, and created H.P. Products in 1945 to sell the trains and track. Lionel made its big break with O gauge, offering a line of OO gauge trains that were slightly larger than HO, with the distance between the track rails measuring 0.75 inch (2cm), compared to HO's 0.65 inch (1.65cm). Lionel made its move by simply "borrowing" and then licensing parts from the Scalecraft Company, which had pioneered the gauge. Lionel's OO gauge, Hudson 4-6-4, die-cast locomo-tive was an exquisite model that was expensive but very well received. Unfortunately, Lionel promptly shot itself in the foot by building a second model Hudson designed to run on its new three-rail, OO gauge track. Lionel's three-rail

miniature track was a huge marketing blunder that defeated the whole "scale realism" concept. Lionel's OO gauge trains disappeared in 1941.

This confluence of miniature gauge introductions was an attempt by the manufacturers to encourage model hobbyists to buy trains all year long. To the toy train manufacturers' dismay, their sortie into miniatures flopped and their larger toy trains continued to be a seasonal item that put a year's sales expectations into one throw of the dice over the winter holidays.

By the 1939 catalog, American Flyer's first O gauge ³⁄₁₆-inch (0.48cm) scale offerings were introduced and the HO trains slipped to the back pages. Gilbert would continually flirt with HO trains throughout the company's existence.

As the world of American Flyer was changing, the rest of the world was shifting gears as well. Europe was in turmoil as Germany prepared to march across the Polish border, daring between Britain and France to declare war. The Depression was easing off, as durable-goods production began to climb and many plants began gearing up for likely European war production. In Hollywood, classic films were released, including *Stagecoach*, *The Wizard of Oz*, and *Gone with the Wind*. President Roosevelt was running for an unprecedented third term in office and Joe Louis beat "Two-ton" Tony Galento in the fourth round in Yankee Stadium.

Ogden Coleman, his wife, Rowena, and their daughter, Kirby, left for New Orleans on March 1, 1939, with their Winnetka neighbors, Mr. and Mrs. Hill Black. Ogden's health had deteriorated due to severe gastric problems and once again he needed a rest. In New Orleans, they boarded the United Fruit Line ship *Loloa*, bound for Antigua in Guatemala. It was a long, leisurely cruise aboard a banana boat fitted with luxury cabins. They docked and were driven to the city of Antigua, where Ogden Coleman's family health history would catch up with him.

On a warm evening in an Antiguan supper club, Ogden asked Rowena for a dance. A few minutes later, young Kirby noticed a disturbance on the dance floor. Ogden Coleman, at age forty-seven, had collapsed and died of heart failure. His grandmother, Julia, had died of heart failure in 1876 at age thirty-seven. William Ogden Coleman Sr. had been fifty-four

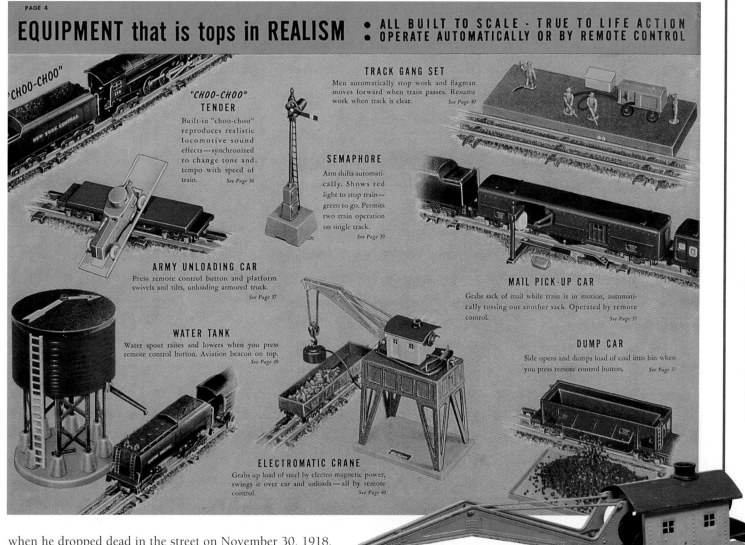

PAGE 4

EQUIPMENT that is tops in REALISM • ALL BUILT TO SCALE - TRUE TO LIFE ACTION • OPERATE AUTOMATICALLY OR BY REMOTE CONTROL

"CHOO-CHOO"

"CHOO-CHOO" TENDER

Built-in "choo-choo" reproduces realistic locomotive sound effects—synchronized to change tone and tempo with speed of train. *See Page 36*

TRACK GANG SET

Men automatically stop work and flagman moves forward when train passes. Resume work when track is clear. *See Page 40*

SEMAPHORE

Arm shifts automatically. Shows red light to stop train—green to go. Permits two train operation on single track. *See Page 39*

ARMY UNLOADING CAR

Press remote control button and platform swivels and tilts, unloading armored truck. *See Page 37*

MAIL PICK-UP CAR

Grabs sack of mail while train is in motion, automatically tossing out another sack. Operated by remote control. *See Page 37*

WATER TANK

Water spout raises and lowers when you press remote control button. Aviation beacon on top. *See Page 40*

DUMP CAR

Side opens and dumps load of coal into bin when you press remote control button. *See Page 37*

ELECTROMATIC CRANE

Grabs up load of steel by electro magnetic power, swings it over car and unloads—all by remote control. *See Page 40*

TOP: In 1941, A.C. Gilbert was producing numerous action cars and accessories to add "play value" to the new scale model trains running on O gauge track. This catalog sent American parents to the toy stores just before the outbreak of World War II in the United States. All toy train production was halted for the duration of the war.

BOTTOM: This prewar version of the Electromagnetic Crane dates from 1939 to 1942 and differs from its postwar cousins, which were produced from 1946 to 1953, with its black (instead of silver) base. The Model 583 was a popular American Flyer accessory that sold as well as it worked. Many a young person improved their eye-hand coordination with this toy when they used the magnetic crane to load metal scrap into gondolas.

when he dropped dead in the street on November 30, 1918. Ogden Coleman passed away on March 13, 1939.

Coleman's body was cremated in Antigua, after which Rowena charted a plane and flew back to Winnetka with her daughter and her husband's ashes to prepare for memorial services. Ogden's widow would live in Hadhisway Hall on Meadow Lane until her death at age eighty-nine.

Coleman's death seemed to sever the last connection to the old American Flyer plant on Halsted Street in Chicago. The company's history would now be forged in New Haven, Connecticut. Though many employees made the trip east from Chicago, there was no mistaking who was in charge of Flyer's future. A.C. Gilbert and American Flyer were in it together.

All the American Flyer tools and dies for the 1938 line were shipped from Chicago in January and February, with

AMERICAN

FLYER

TOP: The last American Flyer catalog using the old Flyer logo was printed in 1938 and featured remaining O gauge inventory and new scale models being built in New Haven, Connecticut, by A.C. Gilbert.

OPPOSITE: Along with the excellent 1936 die-cast Hudson and graceful Pensy "torpedo" steamer, American Flyer in Chicago built an elegant little 0-6-0 switcher in 1938 modeled after the ubiquitous Pennsylvania Railroad B-6 prototype. This O gauge Model 4321 has realistic drive-rod action, scale proportions, and towed a step-back tender. However, there is no front coupler, which makes for difficult yard-switching.

the key employees leaving in April. Young women were hired right out of school with no experience working in a factory. New employees had to be trained and conveyor lines needed to be built. Even though construction was going on, locomotives, cars, and accessories had to be assembled and packaged for the 1938 Christmas season.

Gilbert wasted no time in developing the new product line. One of the lead employees to make the journey to New Haven in 1938 was Guy Schumacher, factory manager for Chicago American Flyer. Well aware of the need for considerable advance work when introducing a new line of products, he plunged right in. Prototype locomotive plans were consulted and drawings were generated in ³⁄₁₆-inch (0.48cm) scale. The drawings were broken down to determine what processes currently available could handle the work and what new processes had to be created. For each locomotive

and car, a model was made to determine the number of parts needed and which ones required casting in zinc alloy. With the parts count finished and costs determined, Schumacher and his staff began generating the drawings for tools and dies. All the production work—including the zinc die-casting—was done on site at the Gilbert plant. A run of twelve to twenty-four pieces was completed for inspection by the engineers and designers; then any necessary changes were made. Following that inspection, another run of a thousand pieces raced through the plant to see if there were any production problems or bottlenecks.

Finally, all parts were scheduled over a six-month basis, with parts fabrication planned one month before the assembly schedule. Expeditors followed the production process, which included virtually all die-casting, 100 percent of metal fabricating, 80 percent of plastic molding, and 60 percent of

NEW CHALLENGERS OF THE HIGH IRON

TRU-MODEL TRAINS OF TOMORROW

AS SHOWN AT THE NEW YORK WORLD'S FAIR 1939

GILBERT AMERICAN FLYER ELECTRIC TRAINS

screw-machine parts. Gilbert needed to purchase some parts, too, during the latter part of the Depression, as a hedge against any further financial surprises that would leave him with too many machines for too little work.

This rapid turnaround in 1938, in order for the company to create the new line in time for 1939, may have caused the corrosion—discovered years later by collectors—of those early die-castings. Minute quantities of cadmium, lead, or tin impurities in the zinc alloy caused the casting to warp and crack through an electrochemical reaction called "intergranular corrosion." It's not hard to imagine the frantic pace required to meet all the new product-scheduling deadlines as well as turn out the products designed for 1938.

Recognizing the huge commitment needed to move an entire plant from Chicago to New Haven, create a new line of die-cast scale models, and present these complex toys to the buying public within the period of one year makes Gilbert's achievement all the more amazing.

TOP: A full lineup of American Flyer steam engines graces the cover of the 1939 catalog that was sent in huge batches to the World's Fair. A 4321 semiscale switch engine is just behind the Fair's Trylon and Perisphere logo. The ³⁄₁₆-inch (0.48cm) scale Northern (called the Challenger) is next to the Hudson 4-6-4, and taking up the back track is the 420 steam double-header set from Chicago Flyer inventory.

AMERICAN

FLYER

BORDEN'S MILK CAR

BUILT BY AMERICAN FLYER LINES

The 1939 American Flyer catalog announced the sweeping changes in the company's product line in a forty-eight-page display catalog printed in black, white, and yellow, the same look as the interim 1938 book. By constrast, all the Chicago American Flyer catalogs had been in full color. It's possible that the printing budget was cut back to cover the costs of advertising, moving, installation of the Chicago assets, and building the new trains, but this lapse in image hardly made for a brilliant showcase for the new products. To offset the less-than-impressive catalog design, Gilbert had a huge number of catalogs printed and made sure a batch showed up at the World's Fair in New York.

If there was any question that American Flyer was still in competition for department store shelf space, the landmark 1939 catalog showed fresh, new ideas and made no bones about who was now in charge. The catalog opened with thirteen pages of prototype railroad photos—all taken of the New Haven Railroad near Gilbert's plant. A photo of A.C. Gilbert himself, with a boy wearing knickers and John Kane, an engineer at the New Haven plant, appears on the second page. They are standing in front of a big I-5 1400 series Hudson, one of ten built by the Baldwin Locomotive Works of Philadelphia, Pennsylvania, in 1937 and streamlined with a steel shroud. On that same page is mentioned the Gilbert

OPPOSITE BOTTOM: This Model 412 Borden's milk car, a similar car to the 3212 car shipped out in 1936, was offered in 1939. Type 8 trucks support a black frame and the white tank. Note that this car has the new link couplers of the A.C. Gilbert era.
BOTTOM: This head-on view of a 1939 vintage American Flyer steam engine, provides a look at the smoke box and huge headlight that were part of the Type 10 die-cast boiler.

Hall of Science, later to become a national icon for progressive design ideas.

American Flyer's new Remote Directional Control (RDC) system was touted on page 3. Locomotives could be reversed anywhere on the track from a control button that caused a spurt of DC current to be squirted down the track, activating the reverse mechanism. Any engine that used the RDC no longer required the old reversing lever atop its boiler or roof.

By pages 4 and 5, a "talking train station" made its debut under the name a-KOOSTIKIN Talking Station. Also featured were the "automatic remote control whistle," housed in a billboard at trackside and triggered by a button. The billboard art showed a Royal Typewriter advertisement. An "automatic electric coupler"—Flyer's new "link" couplers—could be opened when moving over a special track section.

The last pages of the opening thirteen-page spread featured an electromagnetic crane that lifted scrap into gondolas, beating Lionel's crane to market by more than a year. And then the book opened up to show the new trains.

Two new locomotives headed the roster. They were the vanguard of what by 1940 would amount to eight 3/16-inch (0.48cm) scale locos running on three-rail, O gauge track. A New York Central 4-6-4 Hudson towed a twelve-wheel coal tender. The boiler was a one-piece die-casting unit that had none of the compressed toy look. Drivers were spoked and "driven" by complex side rod gear and working crossheads at the pistons. Curiously, the 5640 Hudson engine shown in the early catalogs was actually a Lionel 700E, standing in for the American Flyer newcomer.

The other 1939 locomotive was a Union Pacific 4-8-4 steam engine, stretching twenty-one and a half inches (54.6cm) in length. This Northern-type No. 806 was the premier locomotive of the Flyer line and would retain that coveted position even into the postwar period. The cost of its passenger set—$17.50 more than any other O gauge Flyer train set—was obviously aimed at the top of the market.

Accompanying the new die-cast locomotives was a small collection of die-cast freight cars: a stock car, a box car, a tank car, a wrecking car, and a gondola. All the new rolling stock and the locomotives came either finished or as kits, complete with paint and decals.

Throughout all the ballyhoo about the new locos and cars in the 1939 catalog, they were never referred to as 3/16-inch (0.48cm) scale models, but as "Tru-Models," a name that would continue through the line's introduction. Also called Tru-Models were Gilbert's HO trains, among the first to be offered in kit form (to appeal to hobbyists). In the 1939 catalog they slipped to the back pages.

With all the gears turning and Gilbert American Flyer launched, A.C. himself chose the spring of 1939 to vacation on the Alaska Peninsula with his wife, Mary, and some friends. While Mary remained in Anchorage, Gillbert sent people ahead to set up a hunting camp, then followed in a plane chartered from Woodly Airways. The party hunted brown bears and Gilbert bagged a ten-foot (3m) specimen, winning the Clark Trophy for the best North American Big Game shot that year. On their way back, they had to fly though the ash cloud sent up by an erupting volcano, Mt. Veniaminof.

Within three weeks of returning to New Haven, A.C. was on a plane back west to Gambia Bay in the Admiralty Islands for a camera hunt aboard a friend's yacht. He fished for salmon and photographed wildlife for weeks before traveling to Vancouver on August 25. From there, he flew back to New Haven.

All these strenuous adventures almost put an end to the story of Gilbert American Flyer in 1939. When A.C. returned, he came down with double pneumonia and dry pleurisy, also called "devil's grip," a contagious viral infection that causes knifelike pains in the muscles of the chest or upper abdomen. He also contracted empyema, a condition that causes restrictions in lung movement due to a draining of pus into the pleural cavity. Each of the three conditions can be fatal. After spending three months in the New Haven hospital, tended by six nurses, he then required a long period of convalescence that lasted well into 1940.

While A.C. battled his illnesses away from the plant, the people at Gilbert American Flyer pushed ahead with the 1940 line of 3/16-inch (0.48cm) scale models, bringing out an improved version of the 1939 Hudson by adding a new worm gear-drive motor and some casting adjustments. This No. 531 Hudson was complemented by a similarly upgraded

AMERICAN

FLYER

TOP: Just to show that American Flyer is alive, in 2001 Lionel issued a model of the famed "Erector Radio Tower," which was a famous landmark outside the New Haven, Connecticut, plant. A.C. Gilbert achieved early fame as a toy maker with his 1913 toy, the Erector Set. It went on to be a best-seller for decades.

OPPOSITE: A boxed HO gauge "Tru-Model" Hudson "Locomotive & tender kit w/remote directional control." All the parts needed to build the die-cast engine and tender are included, right down to the paint bottles. This kit was available from 1938 to 1941. Gilbert was reaching for the year-round hobby market with the HO gauge kits, but had too big a company for the profits generated by so small a line.

No. 534 Union Pacific 4-8-4 Northern steam engine, complete with die-cast tender.

To round out the fleet, three new locomotives emerged, all of which—like the 4-8-4 Northern—would become American Flyer signature designs. The first was the No. 545 die-cast Atlantic 4-4-2. It came with a Chicago-designed No. 421 tender—noteworthy for its out-of-scale grab-irons—and no special features other than its headlight. Of all the locomotives built by Gilbert, the Atlantic-type was the most reproduced model.

Using the same boiler casting as the Atlantic, Gilbert began its stubborn commitment to modeling unusual railroad prototypes. Instead of remaking the popular Pennsylvania Railroad K-4 Pacific type, American Flyer rolled out the 4-6-2 K-5. The Flyer K-5's chunky boiler looked better above the three drivers than above the Atlantic's two. This locomotive would be the subject of a legal battle between Lionel and American Flyer later on.

Of all the 1940 locomotives, American Flyer Nos. 553 and 556 took the prize. They were "torpedo" shrouded steamers. The 553 was an Atlantic 4-4-2, colored gun-metal gray, using all die-cast parts. Its sister locomotive was, arguably, the most beautiful American Flyer engine ever designed, the Royal Blue. Those words were decaled on the sides of the dark blue locomotive, just above the 4-6-2 Pacific wheel arrangement. This beautiful loco—based on B&O's deluxe line—pulled a string of scale-model 495B passenger coaches and a 490B baggage car. When it was offered in 1941, it gave owners an eye-catching passenger train to stop at their "talking station."

Another breakthrough in 1940 was American Flyer's purchase of a patent granted on November 23 to an independent inventor named Otto Bastiansen for a device Flyer called "Choo-choo." Essentially, Choo-choo was a noisemaker that was supposed to sound like a steam engine puffing along. Initially, the Choo-choo mechanism was fitted into a coal tender like the 563C with a center rail electrical pick-up that powered the Choo-choo motor. Underway, the motor drove a set of gears that moved a plunger, creating the sound. Lionel had produced a "chugger" that sounded like ice clanking in a martini shaker, so now American Flyer had achieved parity.

As the toy train wars between Lionel and American Flyer settled into dueling chuggers, A.C. Gilbert was back on his feet in 1941 and working on a long-range plan for his manufacturing group that included American Flyer. Remember: A.C. was not strictly a train guy. He considered himself an appliance manufacturer who also made toys. His wide-ranging offerings included a full line of household appliances, in addition to chemistry sets, Erector sets, and Mysto Magic sets. He was also a realtor, a builder, a conservationist, and a clubman, constantly seeking positions of recognition in the

Eastern establishment, far away from his Oregon roots. Even the story about how he got the idea for the Erector Set by observing girder work during rides on the New Haven railway was a fabrication. American Flyer historian Andy Jugle has photos of a bridge located in Salem, Oregon—a place A.C. knew well—whose girders match very closely the girders used in Gilbert's Erector patents. Though it's no longer used, the single-track bridge still stands today.

To solidify his Eastern bona fides, A.C. inquired about a building he saw regularly in downtown Manhattan, located on Twenty-fifth Street between Broadway and Fifth Avenue. The building became available in 1941, so A.C. took a five-year lease on the six-story structure for an annual rental fee of $15,000 a year. It became the first Gilbert Hall of Science. A.C. Gilbert Company vice president Herman Trisch converted the space according to A.C.'s ideas, and when the work was finished, William "Bill" Perry, a longtime A.C. Gilbert associate, was placed in charge of all six floors of display and demonstration space. Perry was the ideal manager and greeter, referred to by employees and visitors alike as "the kind man with the white hair."

A.C. Gilbert was not alone in having a showroom in the neighborhood. Lionel had one on the second floor at 15 East Twenty-fifth Street, a half block away. Louis Marx maintained an impressive display space high above the street at 200 Fifth Avenue. That building had been the prime spot for toy manufacturers for years. Even Old Man Ives had thought it prudent to rent a space there, until bankruptcy brought his company down. But of all the toy peddlers, only A.C. Gilbert had his own building.

There were two entrances to Gilbert's building, one on Broadway and the other on Fifth Avenue. Bruce D. Manson and Maury Romer feel those two doors represent two facets of A.C.'s character: Broadway for the showman and Fifth Avenue for the businessman.

Whatever his motive, A.C. was on hand when his brainchild opened on September 17, 1941. At the dedication, he said, "To the boys and girls of America. The Gilbert Hall of Science is yours from this hour on. For me, it is a dream come true—for you I hope it will be an inspiration, a guiding line in the middle of that road which is seldom smooth that

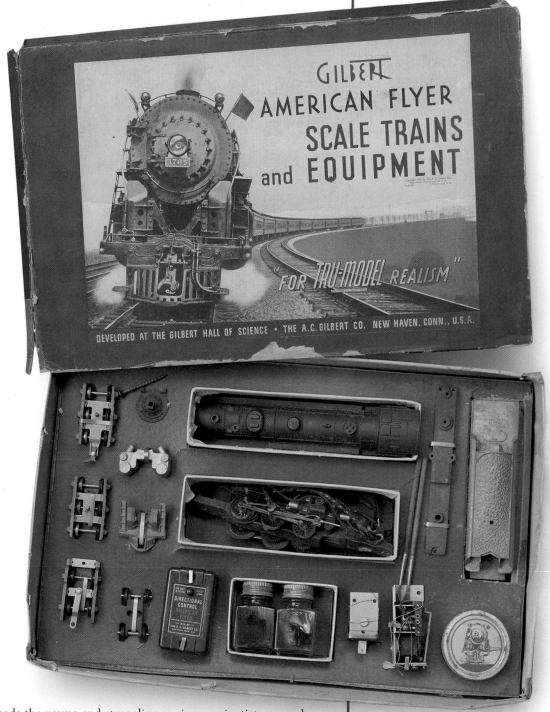

leads the young and struggling engineer, scientist, research worker . . . to that goal which is success. That success at the end of the road to every boy and girl who grows to manhood and womanhood studying and learning, ever striving, is the only true success. Every student and builder who works for the sake of humanity finds at the end that he has worked mightily for himself too. The Gilbert Hall of Science is dedicated to the boys and girls of America forever."

AMERICAN

FLYER

A.C. opened the building to a throng of children who had been shepherded there for the event from the Madison Square Boys Club. They poured in to observe and interact with the products and futuristic philosophy of the A.C. Gilbert Company. And, of course, the tour included a display of American Flyer trains clicking around an O gauge layout near the Fifth Avenue entrance. On display were all the ³⁄₁₆-inch (0.48cm) scale Tru-Model trains *choo-chooing* over an elaborate track setup. Nearby was another layout featuring the HO line. This layout was activated by a "push-me" button. Many parts of the displays invited interaction.

On shelves and tables around the train display room were arrayed all the products for close-up examination. The big difference between the Gilbert Hall of Science and, say, Lionel's showroom down the street was that you could actually buy what you saw on the spot. Your order was taken by a sales representative, sent downstairs to the basement for packaging, then returned for pick-up when your order number was called. The basement was also decorated for entertaining out-of-town buyers and dignitaries. Naturally, all the decorations had a railroad theme.

Traveling upward, the third floor housed the main toy showroom, where Erector was the star, and on the fourth floor, a wide range of kitchen and work appliances were available for demonstration. None of the demonstration areas above the ground floor were open to the public.

A.C. took great pride in his Hall of Science. He wrote in his autobiography, *The Man Who Lives in Paradise*, "It was a wonderful thing to drive [down] Broadway or Fifth Avenue and see the Gilbert Hall of Science, and I still get a big thrill from seeing it in such a

TOP: Still working with inexpensively printed catalogs, Gilbert turned out this 1940 black, white, and yellow version showing a steam maintenance yard. Tooling up the new line of trains at the Connecticut factory was expensive.

BOTTOM: A 4-8-4 Northern *choo-choos* across a red, white, and blue background and past the towering Gilbert Hall of Science in downtown New York City. This 1941 "fine scale model hot shot" would roll into the roundhouse for the war's duration.

AMERICAN

FLYER

prominent place. But the big moment was when we opened it officially with 1,500 boys as guests, and I dedicated it to the boys of America."

So Gilbert stood amid the crowds of boys on opening day, passing out sandwiches and grinning like a kid himself. Flashbulbs popped, the press was impressed, and he was a few more steps removed from his rural Oregon background. He had about three months to savor American Flyer's new

prominence in the toy train marketplace and his own ascension to a high-profile position in New York's wheeler-dealer society. The Erector sets and Mysto Magic sets had started him on his way, but he had owned those markets. Now, he was taking on Joshua Lionel Cowen, who was himself a force of nature and had the scars to prove it. A.C. Gilbert had never failed at anything he attempted and Cowen was aware of his opponent's strengths. The stage was set for a toy train

This prewar catalog page shows some of the variety of American Flyer's new scale model rolling stock, which featured new Gilbert link couplers. The couplers worked well, but did not look real, a fault that would haunt Flyer's postwar market battle with Lionel.

PAGE 38

No. 476 GONDOLA CAR $2.00
Pressed Steel. Sturdily built with brake wheel. 7⅞" long.

No. 512 TANK CAR $4.00
Die-cast, rails, ladder, simulated filler cap. Car 7½" long.

No. 508 HOPPER CAR $4.00
Die-cast, nickel journal boxes, ladder. Car 6½" long.

No. 482 LOG CAR $2.00
Pressed Steel. Six realistic logs and brake wheel. 7⅞" long.

No. 483 GIRDER CAR $2.00
Pressed Steel. Loaded with bridge girder. Has brake wheel, 7⅞" long.

No. 486 HOPPER CAR $2.00
Pressed Steel. Ladders, brake wheel and manual control lever. 6½" long.

No. 480 TANK CAR $2.00
Pressed Steel. Ladders, hand rail and brake wheel. 7⅞" long.

No. 488 FLOODLIGHT CAR $3.00
Pressed Steel. Light turns and tilts on swivel base. 7⅞" long.

No. 504 GONDOLA CAR $4.00
Die-cast, nickel journal boxes, brake wheel. Car 7½" long.

3/16" SCALE MODEL ROLLING STOCK
to give your railroad resplendent realism

Designed from actual railroad blueprints, these fine pressed steel and die-cast cars are correctly scaled to the most minute detail by painstaking American Flyer engineers. Brake wheels, ladders, journal boxes and even rivet heads are exact miniatures of the real thing. All cars are equipped with automatic couplers. Make a list of the cars you need, then add a new car every month. Cars finished in vivid colored enamel.

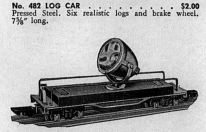

No. 478 BOX CAR $2.00
Pressed Steel. Sliding doors, ladder and brake wheel. 7⅞" long.

No. 516 CABOOSE $4.50
Die-cast. Illuminated. Nickel journal boxes. Car 6" long.

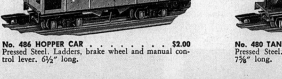

No. 484 CABOOSE $2.00
No. 484L CABOOSE (with light) $2.25
Pressed Steel. Cupola, end rails, ladders. 6½" long.

No. 521 BAGGAGE AND CLUB CAR $5.50
Die-cast. Illuminated. Sliding and hinged doors. 12 wheels. Car 12" long. Finished in green.

No. 524 PULLMAN CAR $5.50
Die-cast. Illuminated. Hinged doors. Car 12" long. Finished in green.

No. 514 WRECKER CAR $5.00
Die-cast. Cab and boom turn on swivel. Boom and hook raises and lowers. Car 7½" long.

No. 506 BOX CAR $4.00
Die-cast, sliding doors, ladder. Car 7½" long.

No. 510 CATTLE CAR $4.00
Die-cast, sliding door, brake wheel, ladder. Car 7½" long.

No. 481 WRECKER $3.50
Pressed Steel. Cab and boom turns on swivel base. Boom and hook raises and lowers. 7⅞" long.

Form 740

THE A. C. GILBERT COMPANY
New Haven, Conn.

AMERICAN FLYER DIVISION CONSUMER PRICE LIST

January 15, 1942

Since this catalog was printed some prices have increased caused by the increased cost of labor, materials and taxes. Please consult prices given below.

4101	Train	$ 8.95
4102	Train	9.95
4103	Train	10.95
4104	Train	11.95
4105	Train	12.95
4106	Train	13.95
4107	Train	14.50
4108	Train	15.50
4109	Train	15.95
4110	Train	15.95
4111	Train	17.95
4112	Train	17.95
4113	Train	19.50
4114	Train	19.95
4115	Train	19.95
4116	Train	21.50
4117	Train	21.50
4118	Train	23.95
4119	Train	23.95
4120	Train	26.50
4121	Train	27.50
4122	Train	27.50
4123	Train	29.50
4124	Train	29.50
4125	Train	34.50
4126	Train	34.50
4127	Train	35.00
4128	Train	35.00
4129	Train	37.50
4130	Train	40.00
4131	Train	40.00
4132	Train	45.00
4133	Train	45.00

3/16" SCALE DIE CAST TRU-MODEL KITS FOR O GAUGE

K559	Penn. K5 Loco. & Tend.	12.50
K531	N. Y. C. Hud. Loco. & Tend.	17.50
K534	U. Pac. Loco. & Tender	22.50
K504	Gondola Car	3.00
K506	Box Car	3.00
K508	Hopper Car	3.00
K510	Cattle Car	3.00
K512	Oil Car	3.00
K514	Wrecker Car	4.00
K516	Caboose	3.50
K521	Baggage and Club	4.50
K524	Pullman	4.50

TRANSFORMERS—CIRCUIT BREAKERS

5	Transformer 50W-60C	2.75
6	Transformer 75W-60C	3.75
5A	Transformer 50W-25C	3.95
6A	Transformer 75W-25C	5.50
5B	Trans. w/CB. 50W-60C	3.95
7B	Trans. w/CB. 75W-60C	5.50
8B	Trans. w/CB. 100W-60C	6.95
9B	Trans. w/CB. 150W-60C	10.95
12B	Trans. w/CB. 250W-60C	14.50
11	Circuit Breaker	1.75
10DC	DC Inverter	10.95
541	Inverter Fuse	.15
540	Dir. Con. Button	1.50

O GAUGE TRACK EQUIPMENT—CROSSOVER—SWITCHES

681	Straight Track	$ .25
680	Curved Track	.25
621	½ Sec. Straight Track	.25
622	½ Sec. Curved Track	.25
413	12 Steel Track Pins	.15
414	4 Fibre Track Pins	.15
450	Track Terminal	.20
602	Crossover 90°	1.50
604	Train Con. Crossover 90°	3.00
665	Pr. Switch—Manual	3.95
688	Pr. Switch—Remote	8.95
675	Remote Control Uncoupler	2.50
676	Pr. Trucks w/Auto. Couplers	.75
677	Auto. Track Trip	.35

O GAUGE EQUIPMENT

247	Tunnel	1.00
248	Tunnel	2.00
577	Remote Con. Whistle	2.95
578	Station Fig. Set	1.75
579	Street Light	1.25
580	Double Arc Light	1.95
581	Girder Bridge	2.25
582	Auto. Blinker Set	1.95
583	Electromatic Crane	5.95
584	Bell Danger Signal	3.95
585	Tool Shed	1.25
586F	Wayside Station w/Fig.	2.25
587	Block Signal	3.95
588	Auto. Semaphore	4.95
589	Pass. & Frt. Station	3.95
591	Crossing Gate Set	3.95
593	Signal Tower	2.95
594	Track Gang Set	4.95
595	Tool Shed (a-Koostikin)	6.95
596	Water Tank	3.95
597	P. & F. Sta. (a-Koostikin)	9.95
598	a-Koostikin Record	.35
610	Bumper w/Track	1.00
611	Trestle Bridge	2.50
612	Station w/Crane	4.95

PKGS. LAMPS—Packed 1 to Pkg.—12 Pkgs. to Carton

440	14V Rd. Clear	.25
441	14V Rd. Red	.25
443	14V Rd. Green	.25
451	14V Frosted w/Cap	.25
452	14V Train Lamp Min.	.50

LOCOMOTIVE AND TENDER SETS WITH BUILT-IN CHOO-CHOO—BELL

556-555C	B & O Loco. and Ten.	11.00
565-564C	Atlantic Loco. and Ten.	13.00
561-558C	Penn. Loco. and Ten.	16.00
559-558C	Penn. Loco. and Ten.	21.00
570-563C	Hudson Loco. and Ten.	21.00
531-563C	Hudson Loco. and Ten.	26.00
572-567C	U. P. Loco. and Ten.	26.00
534-567C	U. P. Loco. and Ten.	31.00
574B-573B	Nickel Plate Loco. and Ten.	19.00
575B-576B	Yard Goat Loco. and Ten.	24.00

showdown when the Japanese attacked Pearl Harbor. Suddenly, the United States was at war.

Virtually all U.S. toy manufacturing stopped as Americans waded into World War II. The U.S. Army was ranked just barely among the top twelve armies in the world. The U.S. Navy consisted of a handful of aircraft carriers and support ships. The U.S. Army Air Forces were flying P-40 Tomahawks, Brewster Buffalos, F3F Wildcats, and Dauntless Devastators, all underpowered and undergunned. And there was not just one war to be fought, but two—in Europe and in the Pacific.

President Franklin Roosevelt told the world America would build 50,000 airplanes over the next year. Hermann Goering, the head of Germany's Luftwaffe, laughed out loud over Berlin radio in response. The U.S.A. produced 100,000 airplanes; two years later, Goering could see them for himself.

In 1942, the toy industry was impressed into war service, converting its assembly lines to produce weapons and related supplies, wherever possible. Lionel turned to the production of navigational instruments, as it had in World War I. American Flyer, as part of the A.C. Gilbert Company, stepped into a number of defense programs, including booby traps, parachutes, flares, and fighter plane parts.

Motorists near the Gilbert plant stared in amazement as trucks roared up and down the roads trailing parachutes ballooning out the back to test for weak spots in the nylon canopies. At night, the plant was often illuminated with eerie-colored light, as emergency flare igniters were tested. But that wasn't as jarring as the explosions. In 1943, as the flare program declined, the government switched Gilbert over to "firing devices." This was a euphemism for booby traps and land mines. Gilbert engineers combined the expertise they had garnered through the flare-igniter program with their creative use of deception, acquired by producing their Mysto Magic sets. They built an antipersonnel mine that, when triggered, leapt into the air six feet (1.8m) and then detonated, spraying a wide area with shrapnel. These inventive engineers devised a trip-wire booby trap that exploded when the wire was cut. Over the course of the war, Gilbert produced 80 to 90 percent of these devices for the Allied forces, churning out about twenty-six million units.

During this wartime production, Gilbert was allowed to continue manufacturing its chemistry sets because of their educational potential. This resulted in civilian sales of $2.5 million. The A.C. Gilbert company earned $12 million in 1944, its peak year of wartime work.

One wartime project that had a direct impact on American Flyer was a request from the Curtiss-Wright plant in Buffalo, New York. The airplane manufacturer needed small motors to operate the trim tabs on wing and tail surfaces. Gilbert's engineers turned around a design in seventy-two hours and built some prototypes. After testing on P-40 fighter aircraft, the motors were accepted and five weeks later were rolling off the New Haven assembly lines. Thousands of the motors went on to be installed in Grumman Hellcats and the famous Republic P-47 Thunderbolt fighter-bombers. Interestingly, that same motor formed the primary design adapted to propel American Flyer locomotives after the war. Gilbert's advertising agency lost no time in making the patriotic connection with words and pictures in 1946.

Gilbert's inventive contributions to the war effort—such as creating explosive devices by casting them from zinc, rather than using expensive brass, and reducing the weight of mines for easier and safer handling—earned the company four Army-Navy E awards, the highest civilian manufacturing award. Factory production processes were entirely changed. As A.C. wrote in his autobiography, "We never had to reach an accuracy calling for tolerances of more than .002. In our war work we increased that accuracy ten times, working with tolerances up to .0002 . . . within one tenth of the diameter of a human hair. Not many people had thought that toy manufacturers could do such things."

When the war ended in 1945, the A.C. Gilbert company was in a perfect position to resume its assault on Lionel's toy train dominance. Gilbert's strategy surprised everyone.

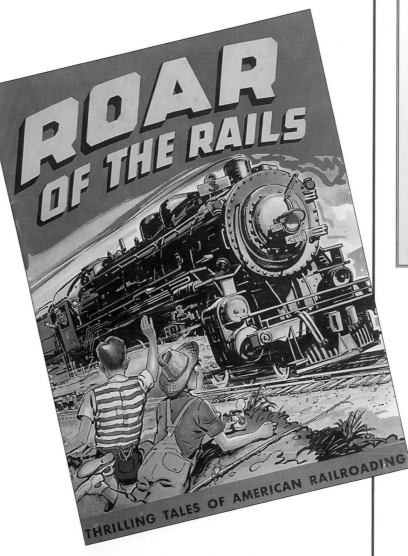

AMERICAN

FLYER

CHAPTER FIVE

A TWO-RAIL ASSAULT

During the war years, the engineers and designers at American Flyer were not just creating clever ways to blow up enemy soldiers or operate wing flaps on fighter planes. They were gearing up for the postwar period with a whole new line of toy trains. This line would be uniquely American Flyer and would set a new toy train standard. Or so they hoped.

During those heady prewar days, when they had hit upon "realism" as their mantra and guiding force, Phil Connell, formerly of Chicago American Flyer, had convinced them that ³⁄₁₆-inch (0.48cm) scale models were the way to go. A.C. had immediately embraced that concept and a lot of money was poured into new tools and dies for a series of steam engines and rolling stock. According to estimates, it took about $100,000 to design, engineer, and tool up for one new locomotive. American Flyer had introduced the Hudson, Atlantic, Northern, 0-8-0 switcher, K-5 steamers, and the Royal Blue between 1938 and 1941.

All the new trains looked as great as they sounded—with their "Choo-choo" noisemakers churning away in their tenders—and they all ran on three-rail track (the industry standard). Even if you owned a Lionel layout, you could still buy an American Flyer engine and cars. The couplers wouldn't match, but a few minutes with a screwdriver, adding new couplers, fixed that. Lionel had finally given up the clumsy latch coupler to install automatic box-and-hook couplers that looked pretty good and were zapped open with an electromagnetic track section. American Flyer introduced a nonprototypical link coupler that uncoupled automatically, worked well, but looked awful when it was uncoupled. The point was that Tommy could

take his American Flyer over to Betsy's Lionel layout and one set of tracks fit all the pieces.

A.C. Gilbert had become enamored with the realism of HO gauge trains running on adult hobbyist layouts. They were scale models and ran on realistic, two-rail track. He had even broached the subject of a Gilbert line of HO trains to Ogden Coleman before the American Flyer takeover had happened. They both agreed that HO was too small and not rugged enough for little kids. But the move to 3⁄16-inch (0.48cm) O gauge had opened the design door. The original 3⁄16-inch (0.48cm) locos and rolling stock Phil Connell had seen in Cleveland ran on S gauge, two-rail track.

S gauge falls almost equally between HO and O gauge in size. The trains Connell had seen were hobby scale models, fussy with details, but their proportions looked absolutely "right." A.C. wanted to capitalize on what he saw as a kid's desire for railroad realism by switching from three-rail to two-rail track. World War II had come along, stopped the "Tru-Model" O gauge production, and given American Flyer breathing room to decide on the new designs. In his autobiography, A.C. put it this way: "Any other line of trains that had been successful is seriously handicapped in making basic changes because the new items may not fit the millions of old trains still in use. That was no problem to us. American Flyer had sold poorly for a few years before we bought it. . . . We could do whatever we wanted."

The Gilbert designers already had their 3⁄16-inch (0.48cm) castings to get the fleet started, as well as die-cast and stamped-steel freight and passenger cars. All they had to do was to squeeze the locos' drivers and the rolling stocks' truck wheels down to fit on S gauge rails, and they were in business. Taking a page from real-world track design, as well as Lionel's track created for the 1937 scale Hudson, American Flyer tinplate, two-rail track had flat-topped rails for better traction. For simplicity, the track was held together with pins fit into the hollow rails and had only four metal cross-ties per section.

By this time, the New Haven plant at the corner of Peck Street and Blatchley Avenue had grown considerably. World War II production had added two buildings to the two that had been built in 1937 when American Flyer came on board.

Now the manufacturing complex sprawled over 12,400 feet of floor space. Employees were pampered with their own recreation area where frequent company meetings were held. A.C. himself kept everyone up to date. Health care programs, day care for employees' children, and a dining room that served good food and could be used as a dance hall and party space were added as employee perks. (The A.C. Gilbert Company was never unionized in A.C.'s lifetime.)

As the last of wartime production left the shops, Gilbert was pressing hard with the retooling to plunge ahead with new two-rail, S gauge trains, but they even went one step further. Since steam engines made up the introductory fleet, it seemed important that they smoke like the real engines. Engineer William R. Smith—called either "Smitty" or "Screwball," depending on the services required—worked with other designers to come up with a smoke unit that fit into the loco's tender with the Choo-choo unit. While the Choo-choo gears ground away, they operated a bellows that blew the smoke through a tube, into the locomotive, to where the smoke puffed from the stack.

The smoke was composed of a mixture of kerosene, mineral oil, and a pine or cedar scent. The "secret" formula was revealed when one mother called in, saying her kid had swallowed one of the plastic ampules containing the smoke fluid. "Smitty" revealed to her that the mineral oil compound was harmless—which, of course, it wasn't. Swallowing any petroleum product can have serious effects, including severe cramps and blindness.

Lionel, meanwhile, had also created a smoke unit. The first device was simply the headlight bulb that was dimpled on top to hold a smoke pill dropped down the stack. This was replaced by a tiny hotplate under the stack that melted a pill made of ammonium nitrate, releasing puffs of nitrogen oxide. The turning drive wheels forced an updraft into the smoke compartment, blowing the whiffs out the stack. The faster the wheels went, the faster the engine puffed.

American Flyer's Choo-choo and smoke were driven by a motor in the tender, which was independent of the engine's speed, so the smoke/Choo-choo effects appeared unrealistic at very slow speeds. However, Flyer engines smoked while standing still, looking very realistic as they built up steam for

TOP: Within the pages of this colorful 1952 catalog, and in the middle of the ballyhoo about Gilbert's full line of toys, was the announcement of real knuckle couplers replacing the old links that had often been airbrushed out of illustrations. Flyer's C&NW 4-6-2 Pacific and the new 4-4-2 Atlantics received plastic boilers, and some passenger cars were now cast in plastic, allowing them to be hauled in longer trains by single motor diesels.

MIDDLE: Paradise Park was created by A.C. Gilbert for his employees from a section of his property. It was the site of picnics, boating, swimming, and hiking. Nearby was the Paradise Game Park, where game birds and critters frolicked for guests until A.C. took down his shotguns in the fall. It was available to Gilbert employees year-round for a $1.50 fee. Members could bring their kids and guests for outings, but big family hoohahs required permission from the Gilbert Director of Recreation. Is it any wonder that A.C. Gilbert's company was never unionized with these kinds of employee perks?

BOTTOM: This ubiquitous little building served many masters. It was the District School in red and white trim with a bell, or the 764 Express Office with gray walls and picture windows. There was also a lightbulb inside.

American Flyer Trains AND **GILBERT TOYS**

The A. C. Gilbert Co.
Erector Square, New Haven, Conn.

paradise park

APPLIANCES FOR SALE

The main products of the A.C. Gilbert Company—and the chief source from which the company's income was derived—were appliances and toys other than trains. That made Gilbert quite different from its chief competitor, Lionel. Joshua Lionel Cowen and his people tried to expand their line, for instance, with a stereo camera and a spin fishing set, but failed. Gilbert was already a successful appliance and toy manufacturer who brought electric trains into the fold. If you went to the fourth floor of the Gilbert Hall of Science in 1956 you saw an array of appliances that were popular at the time.

You could make a Manhattan or a milk shake with the Model B2 drink mixer, and while you waited, your life partner might give you a massage with the Gilbert Vitalator that strapped to the back of his or her hand (the Model 12 had a high speed that some said could shake the fillings out of your teeth). On a counter across the aisle was the Gilbert B29 mixer on its stand, complete with a set of bowls, a juicer, and other kitchen tools. There was also the Gilbert Whirlbeater, a hand-held twin beater for batter, and the single Whirlbeater to mix drinks. The Gilbert hand-held hair dryer "delivered a high volume of hot or cold air" according to the direction sheet and had a heavy detachable base if you didn't feel like holding it.

With your hair dry and thirst slaked, you could drill a hole in the wall with the Gilbert Hobby Electric drill, then suck up the mess with the Gilbert Hand Vacuum Cleaner.

Among the best-selling products were the Polar Cub fans, which ranged in size and velocity from window units to the "Little Giant" Model A410 floor model. The fans were outsold only by the line of Gilbert vibrators.

A.C. Gilbert knew the AC electrical marketplace and had year-long sales to balance the seasonal appeal of his American Flyer trains.

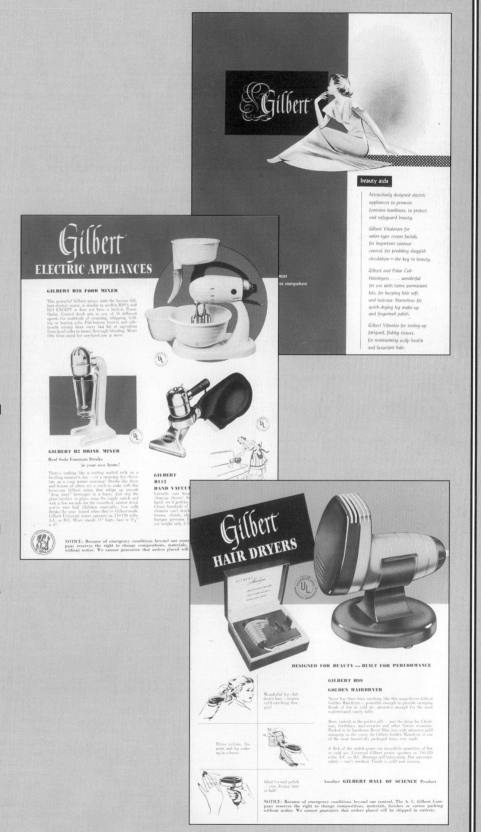

TOP: Beside toys, A.C. Gilbert manufactured a line of beauty aids from vibrators to hair dryers. Nothing better than spending a day running trains, then toning up "fatigued and flabby tissues" with a Gilbert vibrator massage.

MIDDLE: Mixers and vacuum cleaners could also be found on display in Gilbert's Hall of Science. A.C. Gilbert was referring to this line when he said, "I'm an appliance manufacturer who also makes toys."

BOTTOM: This catalog from the mid-1950s shows a futuristic hair/nail dryer design that is "another Gilbert Hall of Science product." Profits generated by these lines were dragged down by the underperforming toy trains as the turbulent '60s loomed.

The 4-8-4 Northern Model 332 from 1948 was a major American Flyer accomplishment—a steam locomotive in scale proportions. Its eight drive wheels are driven though an L-shaped crosshead, which made for great steam action. The Challenger name was misleading, however. The real Challenger is a 4-6-6-4 articulated locomotive created for the Union Pacific Railroad. This version of a Northern type was a uniquely American Flyer locomotive.

their next trip. Both Lionel and American Flyer premiered their smoky locos on the same day in New York. Lionel smoked up its showroom on Twenty-fifth Street. Gilbert chose to show off its pungent engines in the second floor dealer's showroom at the Hall of Science.

For the big premiere, American Flyer added smoke to four of its five prewar locomotives, now running on S gauge track. The AF Atlantic 4-4-2 was released without a smoke unit as a lower-cost motive power option. Eventually, all the locos were sold with or without smoke.

Even though the company had done all the preparation and had new locomotives and rolling stock ready to go at the end of 1945, American Flyer did not release its new line until 1946. That catalog was the largest toy train catalog ever printed, measuring ten and a quarter by twenty-nine inches (26 X 74cm) when opened up. Lionel got a leg up on Gilbert by publishing its entire catalog in a special 1945 edition of *Liberty* magazine. And in that display of products, which were mostly prewar reissues of trains and accessories, one freight set must have come as a shock to the American Flyer people.

A modest Lionel Model 224 die-cast steam engine trailed a string of mostly prewar, stamped-steel freight cars—except

for a die-cast plastic Pennsylvania Railroad gondola—and they were all connected with very realistic knuckle couplers. These couplers could be zapped open when they crossed a special track section and a truck-mounted shoe passed over a fourth rail. While American Flyer touted its two-rail realism and scale-model proportions, those Lionel couplers looked like the real McCoy, compared to AF's link couplers.

One prewar locomotive missing from the 1946 American Flyer lineup was the beautiful Royal Blue. That streamlined steamer did not appear in S gauge until 1948. Another anomaly for 1946 was the use of proto-typical road names on the tenders. Following 1946, the tenders used a road name and logo as a patch below the tenders' coal bins, but either "American Flyer" or "American Flyer Lines" was decaled or stamped where the real-life road name would be found. This practice continued throughout the life of American Flyer trains. Since only Flyer trains ran on their own proprietary two-rail track, did the kids have to be reminded that they were running American Flyer trains?

For all that, the American Flyer locomotives, rolling stock, and accessories that appeared in the postwar

AMERICAN

FLYER

LEFT: Looking at an American Flyer K-5 head-on reveals the "fat" boiler and pilot overhang above narrow S gauge rails. Originally cast in ³⁄₁₆-inch (0.48cm) scale running on O gauge one-and-a-quarter-inch (3cm)-wide three-rail track, Gilbert kept the castings for the narrower gauge to create an "instant" fleet of postwar locos. **BELOW:** The Model 23596 water tank, introduced in 1946, did more than just sit there. When your steamer rolled its tender in place, the spout lowered at the press of a button.

ABOVE AND ON THE FOLLOWING PAGES:
This fifteen-panel adventure was part of a series of four begun in the 1950s. Here, a young engineer sees little criminals on his train set—miniaturized by Professor Carter's secret reducing machine. By using his American Flyer action cars and accessories, Carter's plucky son manages to defeat the nasty little men. The American Flyer Adventure Series came in specially marked boxes of Kellogg's Sugar Corn Pops cereal.

RIGHT TOP: Imagine how a child's heart skipped a beat upon seeing this envelope in the mailbox. Inside was 1946 American Flyer catalog—the largest catalog ever printed by a toy train manufacturer.

RIGHT BOTTOM: Two pals and their loyal Scottish terrier stand close to the crossing gate as a locomotive thunders past. They can't wait to see the wonders offered by American Flyer in this chock-full-of-trains 1946 catalog.

AMERICAN

FLYER

period were exceptional models and added to the prestige of the A.C. Gilbert Company. Many cars incorporated plastic as a value-added feature, but when some of these plastic chassis warped and cracked, they were replaced with die-cast metal in 1947. As plastic formulations improved, more and more metal would be replaced and considerable costs saved.

The very first box car to appear in S gauge was the 1946 No. 633, a brown car wearing B&O livery. You could find it coupled to the No. 625 black Shell tank car, or a No. 628 Chicago & North Western flat car with six logs strapped in place. An Army Searchlight car, No. 634, shined in those early 1946 trains, possibly just ahead of the No. 635 Wrecker Crane with its yellow gear shack and red roof. At the tail end of that freight, maybe just ahead of the No. 632 L&NE gray hopper car, was an illuminated No. 630 Reading caboose. Later, Flyer cabooses were lettered "American Flyer Lines."

Most scale modelers love the proportions of S gauge rolling stock and the American Flyer cars were no exception. When the link couplers were hooked together, the effect wasn't half bad: a long, winding consist clicking along

behind a puffing, choo-chooing, scale locomotive was a thing of beauty. Many lifelong fans of the A.C. Gilbert American Flyer trains were created on the spot. But there could be no letup, no resting on laurels won in the past. American Flyer was definitely in the game for keeps. Over at Lionel, designers and sales staff alike couldn't help but sit up and take notice.

To stir the pot, Gilbert opened another Hall of Science in Washington, D.C., at 1610 K Street NW, a storefront location, on August 1, 1946. As with the New York opening, A.C. was there consecrating the ground with one of his uplifting speeches. American Flyer trains puffed along as A.C. launched into another, "Hello boys and girls!" inspirational chat, directed to the three thousand visitors: "And now—this Gilbert Hall of Science is yours from this hour on. . . . So I want to welcome you here today. I am very happy in doing so . . . because it gives me the chance to meet and speak to the future masters of science."

Gilbert saw these Halls of Science as major showcases for the full range of its products as well as

BOTTOM: This 1946 Model 594 Track Gang went into action as a train approached: the flagman moved forward and the roadbed tampers stepped back. After the train passed, work resumed.

AMERICAN

FLYER

American Flyer trains. The Washington, D.C., location welcomed about five hundred visitors a day for the first few weeks following its opening. A visit there was an outing for the whole family; they could buy as well as look. Later, in 1953, Gilbert opened another Hall of Science in Chicago at 512 South Michigan Avenue in the luxurious Congress Hotel. A portion of the hotel was set aside for a large American Flyer layout; shelves were loaded with Flyer trains and accessories.

Except for the New York Hall of Science, these other Halls, located in very expensive locations, were partnerships. In an arrangement similar to the Congress Hotel partnership in Chicago, the Washington, D.C., store was also privately owned and operated. It wasn't long before large American Flyer display layouts were popping up in department stores from the prestigious FAO Schwarz in New York to Bullock's and the May Company in Los Angeles. Gilbert's marketing people believed the best way to sell Flyer trains was to show kids how good they looked on professionally sculpted layouts and let the imagination do the rest. Virtually every available medium was embraced to tell the two-rail story.

The 1946 catalog acted as a weather vane, pointing the way American Flyer would proceed over the years to come. As with the Flyers of early days, passenger cars were featured prominently. They were offered in five different trains, prototypically long and businesslike. The early heavyweight models came in two basic styles: with six-wheel trucks on the high end and shorter cars with four-wheel freight trucks on the lower-priced sets.

A 4-8-4 Northern—called the Challenger—pulled the Union Pacific No. 4621 set. Five passenger cars trailed behind the big locomotive: an operating mail car that snatched a mailbag from its post as the train rushed past the station, two of the shorter New Haven–type cars with four-wheel trucks, and two of the long, six-wheel Pullmans.

The catalog copywriter almost blew a fuse with his effervescent puffery, describing the Challenger: "Wonder of the West! Watch this mammoth Union Pacific Hotshot hustle its varnish over the rails as smoke pours from its stack and its 'Choo-choos' echo and re-echo." Unless the train was running in a tile bathroom, the echoes were unlikely—but they could be heard in the kid's imagination, trailing back from rocky mountaintops.

The five sets featured in the voluminous 1946 catalog promised a great mix of colorful passenger cars and smoke-puffing engines. Unfortunately, as with future American Flyer catalogs, the blaze of promised railroad excitement fizzled in the face of reality. Some of the passenger sets existed in pictures only. This time, a shortage of critical materials still lingered as the economy shifted from its war footing. Both American Flyer and Lionel were guilty of overpromising and underdelivering in their catalogs. Lionel's huge inventory of offerings, network of dealers, and market dominance offset its occasional marketing gaffes. American Flyer could not afford marketing missteps as it tried to build up its reputation.

Clever accessories for toy train layouts were an American Flyer hallmark from the start. Again, the 1946 catalog set the tone. The prewar No. 583 Electromagnet crane was brought back, selling for two dollars less than its original price of $6.95. This is the crane that beat Lionel to the punch by a year and was a terrific toy. Operating the magnet to lift metal (possibly Gilbert's Erector Set girders) into waiting gondolas, "gives you an uncanny sense of power," promised the ad copy. Operating the magnet and judging its capacity for scrap

were tricky skills to master; the crane boom had to be moved by hand, but "play value" were growing buzzwords and the crane had plenty of that.

Keeping children occupied for hours with their toy train was easy with accessories like the No. 751 Log Loader. This 1946 timber handler lifted logs from one bin and rolled the heavy logs down onto waiting stake-side log cars. It was a large accessory requiring a long siding, but it remained in the line until 1953.

The crowning achievement of American Flyer designers and engineers, most Flyer historians agree, was the Auto-matic Seaboard Coaler that also debuted in 1946. "Up goes the bucket . . . down slides the coal," hyped the catalog copywriter. "What fun it is to load coal cars by remote push-button control." Here again, the reality of operating the Seaboard Coaler was another matter. On the early model, the boom with the bucket at its end scooped coal from a track-side bin, raised the bucket to a bunker and released the coal, which slid down a chute into a waiting hopper or dump car on the adjoining track. This required some degree of prac-ticed dexterity—and a lot of coal to offset spillage. Later, in 1951, the raised bunker received a baffle over the end of the

BOTTOM: American Flyer shipped out the No. 42597 as a log car, but this one has been modified to carry a floodlight. With its ingenious design, the flat car's hauling ability was limited only by the operator's imagination.

BUT AS TERRY PRESSES ANOTHER BUTTON...

OH-H-H... PETE! HE'S GULP... OUT COLD!

CLUNK

AND AS THE STARTLED CHARLIE RACES OFF...

THAT'S IT, DAD... HOP INTO THAT HAND CAR! IT'S THE FASTEST WAY TO GET YOU TO HIM!

HE'S CATCHING UP FAST... GOTTA GET AWAY FROM HERE!

GOOD... THAT WABASH HOPPER IS JUST WHERE I WANT HIM TO GO!

BASH

ANOTHER TURN OF THE TRANSFORMER, AND...

HUH--? WHERE'S THIS THING TAKING ME?

chute that allowed the coal to be stored and released later into a waiting car with the touch of a button.

But these accessories couldn't operate without accompanying action cars. American Flyer provided these in 1946. The No. 716 Automatic Coal Dump car was a departure from the Lionel version that tipped the entire gondola bed to release the coal. The American Flyer model resembled a standard hopper car, but when zapped by an electromagnetic track section, a panel opened along the length of the car and the coal slid down an incline. Each car came with a bag of granule-sized coal.

The log unloader for 1946 was the No. 717. A control button activated a pin in the flat car chassis that pushed up on a sheet-metal platform. The platform tipped up, the stakes along the side tipped down, and the three logs rolled off into a waiting bin. The lifting platform concept was also used in a unique American Flyer car that carried a single vehicle. The 1946 model was black and red and was loaded with an Army scout car made by Tootsietoy. Once positioned over the electromagnetic track, a push of a button activated a solenoid

that caused the platform to rotate. When the platform was at right angles to the car, the vehicle's weight made it tip down so the scout car rolled off into the countryside.

These early action cars, which were gradually modified, matured in concept over the years, but their play value, when combined with accompanying accessories, was a huge factor in keeping American Flyer competitive. From those early postwar days, Flyer designers and engineers created even more ingenious accessories and cars, as technology provided new solutions.

After the big splash in 1946, the next year saw few changes in motive power or rolling stock, but a major change was instituted in the engine power plants: American Flyer switched from AC to DC power. The copywriters pushed the fact that direct current (DC) power gave "smooth direct control," as opposed to the intermittent power afforded by alternating current (AC). Actually, the reverse mechanisms in AC-powered locomotives were in full operation all the time and were becoming magnetized. All the locomotives were not switched over to DC, but the No. 332 Union Pacific

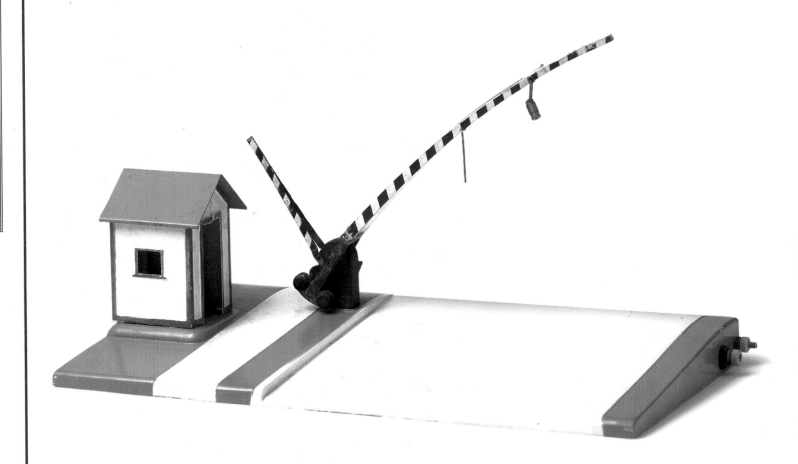

BOTTOM: The very clever 591 crossing gate introduced in 1946 uses realistic-looking skinny parts and a tiny lantern for the gate. When the gate drops, a light shines up through a hole in the road crossing to illuminate the lantern.

OPPOSITE LEFT: The 1949 American Flyer catalog celebrated Gilbert's train and Erector products showing a white-tire Hudson chugging through a sampling of Erector projects, all of them promising "fun & thrills."

OPPOSITE RIGHT: "Sam the Semaphore Man" was a popular Flyer accessory. As the train approaches, you push a button. Sam then emerges from his shack and the semaphore arm drops, revealing a red light. The train stops. Release the button, up goes the arm and Sam pops back in his shack. Created in 1949, Sam became a staple on American Flyer layouts and rug railroads.

Northern and No. 342 nickel plate 0-8-0 heavy switcher were offered as test beds. To convert AC out of the wall socket into DC, Gilbert created a gloriously named "Electronic Rectiformer," using a rectifier tube made by Sylvania to provide "Electronic Propulsion" to these locos. With the Rectiformer connected, both AC and DC trains could still be run and operated independently.

Curiously—and again attesting to the casual approach to accuracy that characterized Flyer catalogs—the 332 UP Northern with DC power apparently was never manufactured.

It also appears that the nickel-plate switcher was not a big seller, because today these trains are very rare. On the plus side, compared to the ghost trains offered in the 1946 catalog, 1947 production did kick in and more cataloged items were actually available for sale.

Another bit of changing technology was previewed in the 1947 catalog. While the locomotives being sold had both Choo-choo and smoke still located in the tender, the instruction manuals listed a variation that had both these features lodged inside the loco's boiler—the shape of things to come.

AMERICAN

FLYER

The year 1948 was super for American Flyer. Superman, the popular comic book hero, joined forces with the A.C. Gilbert ad team. In a special American Flyer catalog that featured Superman on the cover, the superhero says to a pair of awestruck lads watching a locomotive chug past, "Railroading is full of thrilling action and spectacular drama." Dazzled, they reply, "And American Flyers are just like real. The faster they go, the more smoke they puff and the louder the Choo-choos sound."

All this passion was due to the placement of the smoke and Choo-choo units in the locomotive. With these features above the drive wheels, the gears and smoke piston were synchronized with the speed of the engine. This solution was elegant: it eliminated the separate motor in the tender and the long tube to the loco that often became clogged or popped loose. But American Flyer was playing catch-up with Lionel once again. Everyone admitted, however, that American Flyer smoke was much better than the greenhouse gas that belched from Lionel stacks.

As if 1947 had never happened, DC-powered locomotives were "introduced" again in 1948. A new rectifier to convert AC to DC was sent into the world as the catalog

RIGHT: This close-up of the American Flyer shrouded Pacific-type loco—the Royal Blue—shows off its elegant lines. Built to resemble a B&O prototype, the Blue was reintroduced many times and in many colors both in O gauge and S gauge. The loco was never very powerful and was relegated to short passenger trains and freights.

trumpeted the "New! No. 15 Directronic Rectifier." "Electronic Propulsion" became "Directronic Propulsion" and the poor 0-8-0 switcher was sent forth yet again, this time as the No. 342DC.

The beautiful Royal Blue, Pacific-type, streamlined loco was finally added to the S gauge line, but hauling a cheap string of freight cars and without either smoke or Choo-choo. Regardless of all the strangeness, American Flyer posted its biggest sales year in 1948. Production was almost in full swing and the company's designers zeroed in on new ideas to crank up sales even further.

During these early years, the company kept following a pattern of technological epiphanies that came to nothing, coupled with confusing ad copy, which dogged American Flyer throughout its existence. The company had beautiful trains, clever accessories, and a market to nurture over the long run. But American Flyer could not resist the urge to tinker. Sometimes the tinkering produced a great toy, like the "Talking Train Station," reintroduced from prewar days, that stopped the train, played a record of sounds of steam releasing and train calls (ending with "All aboard!") and restarted the train. But at other times, real and imagined products got in the way of the company's mission.

In its zeal to seize a larger chunk of market share, American Flyer charged into 1949 with a little toot that didn't, Sam the Semaphore Man, a propulsion identity crisis, and a torpedo that fizzled.

In 1949 a very realistic-sounding whistle was packed into the innards of American Flyer's K-5 locomotive. The whistle's sound was triggered by a button near the trans-former that sent a squirt of DC current down the track to the AC-powered K-5 and closed a relay in the whistle mecha-nism. Unfortunately, this was exactly the way Lionel trig-gered the whistle it had been using since the late 1930s. A red flag went up. A cease-and-desist letter on Lionel sta-tionery was fired off and the whistle was yanked. American Flyer fell back on its "whistling billboards" that were activat-ed as a train passed them.

The DC Power Follies were still playing out as the origi-nal "Electronic Rectiformer" was resurrected with a redesigned Sylvania tube and "Directronic Propulsion" was

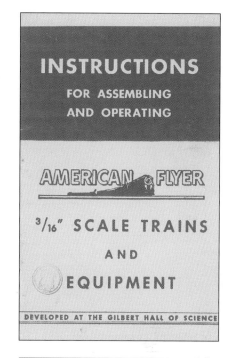

INSTRUCTIONS
FOR ASSEMBLING AND OPERATING

AMERICAN FLYER

3/16" SCALE TRAINS AND EQUIPMENT

DEVELOPED AT THE GILBERT HALL OF SCIENCE

TOP: A 1949 instruction manual refers to "³⁄₁₆" [0.48cm] scale trains" rather than S gauge, a harkening back to the American Flyer "scale model" selling point versus Lionel's truncated trains.

This coal dump car was introduced in 1950 as the Model 719. With the push of a button a solenoid in the car activates a pin that pops up through the frame and tips the loaded coal bin. It originally came with link couplers. This is a later 1954 example with operating knuckle couplers.

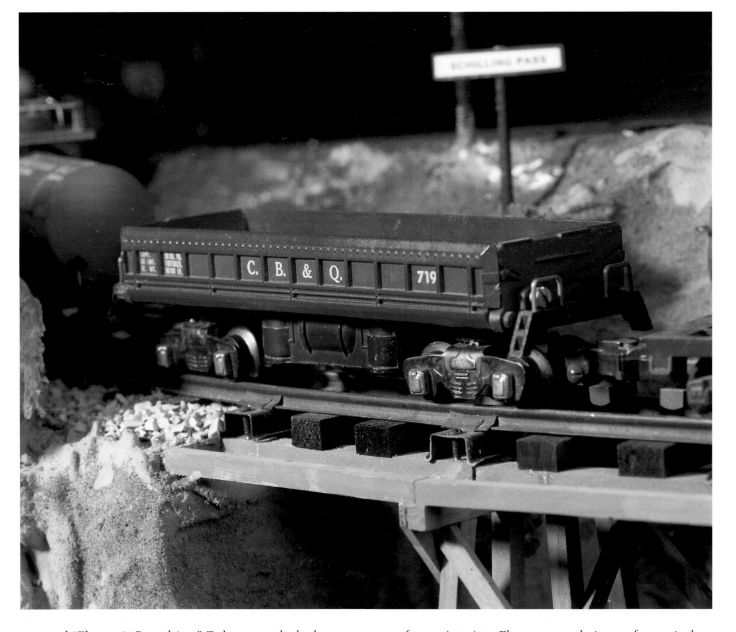

renamed "Electronic Propulsion." To keep everybody thoroughly confused, the "Directronic Rectiformer" of 1948 was kept in the line, providing two ways to control one locomotive no one was buying.

"Sam the Semaphore Man," was a big hit. Sam came out of his little shack with a flag, the semaphore arm dropped, and the train stopped—all at the push of a button. When the button was released, everything returned to its original position and the train restarted. You could just imagine kids battling to see who would push the button next time.

If Sam was a hit, a cataloged "torpedo" was a disappointing no-show. Unfortunately, this kind of thing happened all too often at American Flyer: copy and pictures for particular products went to the catalog printer but those actual products failed to materialize by the time the catalog was published. The No. 760 Track Torpedo was a case in point. The explosive toy was based on actual devices carried by conductors who used them to warn oncoming trains behind theirs that a train was stopped up ahead. The conductor would dash down the tracks and place these pressure activated explosives on the rails. As the American Flyer catalog stated, "two bangs slow trains down and three bangs stop it," adding that this Flyer "remote control" torpedo "uses no explosives and is perfectly safe." Gleeful little kids expecting to set off "perfectly safe" explosions under their locomotives were bafflingly disappointed when this product failed to show up under the Christmas tree.

The here-again-gone-tomorrow Royal Blue locomotive disappeared again in 1949.

But 1949 was just a prelude to the "Fifty Years of Progress" celebration that followed in 1950, a great year for American Flyer hoopla. What "fifty years" they were referring to was a mystery, but the marketers promised "fifty lower prices, fifty exclusive features, and fifty new toys." It was a good *ruse de guerre* to pump up improvements across the entire line.

An AC-powered horn and whistle were introduced, but were yanked near the end of the year as the Korean War absorbed critical parts. Lionel had just introduced Magnetraction in 1950, but had to discontinue it the same year when all aluminum-nickel-cobalt ("alnico") magnets were put on the restricted materiel list. Likewise the horn from the two new diesels that rolled forth from Gilbert's shops was on the restricted list.

Both of these excellent locomotives were victims of the catalog artists, but they were shining examples of the toy train designer's art. A GP-7, in blue and silver Electromotive demonstrator colors, was numbered 370. This road engine was (after the authors' obvious favorite—the Royal Blue) arguably American Flyer's second best-looking locomotive. As realism goes, its proportions were excellent and its potential for a variety of color schemes was huge, since a large

This Model 370 Electromotive GP-7 was available between 1950 and 1953. The train's arrival was a big deal—with its silver-painted plastic shell, head and rear lights, full four-position reverse, and a powerful double worm gear-drive motor. What it didn't have were couplers. Instead, "coupler bars" were offered at either end. American Flyer link couplers simply hooked onto the bars to be towed around. Eventually, as with this example, working knuckle couplers were added, and older models could be retrofitted with the new couplers.

TOP: The elegant prewar Royal Blue streamlined steamer spawned a variety of color schemes. In 1950, the torpedo-nosed loco was splashed in red paint and put at the head end of a circus train. The 353 Pacific-type looked good in any color, but never sold well.

BOTTOM: The American Flyer Circus Train included this Model 643 flat car and load. This is an early 1950 car featuring a red truck and two cages. The cages contained animals and came in a variety of colors. They were produced by Allied Plastics initially, but Gilbert eventually bought the tooling.

OPPOSITE TOP: A Model 360 Santa Fe PA circa 1951 in silver finish with no front coupler rolls past. The Santa Fe locomotive came out in many variations. Its original 1950 version featured a full load of features complete with dual motors for pulling power and a "Nathan Chime" whistle. When introduced, "Santa Fe" was lettered on the sides. This was replaced by "American Flyer Lines" later on, leaving only the Santa Fe logo on the loco's nose.

number of railroads bought this engine. In the catalog, it is shown with link couplers, but the loco that came out of the box only had bars fore and aft for link couplers to hook onto. The trucks were different, too, and there was supposed to be an automatic bell. There was no bell on the production model. Later, when it was installed, it became so annoying that many were disconnected by owners.

The second diesel really charged into Lionel's turf. It was a Santa Fe streamliner, an Alco PA and PB (instead of the brawny F-units hauling Lionel trains). It was a good-looking combination, though you would never know it from the catalog art that omitted a considerable number of details. The actual Flyer PA had custom-made trucks, while the catalog illustration shows what appear to be trucks off a Hudson's tender. This No. 360–361 diesel was the vanguard for an excellent line of diesel streamlined passenger sets in prototypical railroad paint schemes.

Another return visitor was the good old Royal Blue, but this time—besides being painted a darker shade of blue—it was also offered in red. This red, bullet-shaped locomotive headed up a new "Circus Train," complete with decorated cages on flat cars with their truck transport, a searchlight car to let the rubes know the circus was in town, and either a decorated Pullman car or a transfer caboose with side stakes to hold baggage or tent poles. The complete package even had a twenty-seven-piece set of cardboard cutouts for creating a complete circus scene.

This scene concept was further hammered home with a freight hauled by an Atlantic locomotive that also featured a seven-piece farm setup, complete with house, barn, tractor, old hay wagon, and outbuildings.

Improvements in the line included a set of aluminum passenger cars, adding a luxurious Vistadome car and enclosed observation car to a combined baggage-coach and a day coach. The streamlined cars gave the new Santa Fe diesel something to haul, but their weight only allowed the use of three at a time.

A.C. Gilbert's expertise with vibrators in its appliance line worked its way into the No. 771 Stock Yard, accompanied by its No. 736 Stock Car. At the push of a button, the cattle milled (vibrated) around until they followed each

IT'S THE GREAT, NEW GILBERT 1950 TELEVISION CAMPAIGN!

Brand new 15-minute coast-to-coast show, reaching millions of viewers! Televised to 59 cities in the United States — nearly 100% TV saturation! Gilbert program is the "AMERICAN FLYER BOYS' RAILROAD CLUB," featuring American Flyer trains and packing plenty of selling power to boys and their dads—YOUR customers! See list inside for time and station in your area.

A. C. GILBERT COMPANY, Erector Square, New Haven 6, Conn.

BOTTOM: In 1950, Gilbert launched the "American Flyer Boys Railroad Club" coast-to-coast, featuring railroad lore and American Flyer trains. By that time, small-screen television set sales were booming and networks needed programming to build audiences. There were many fifteen-minute programs, and the *Railroad Club* show was a typical offering aimed at kids and was created to sell trains. Lionel's *Tales of the Red Caboose* was a similar program. Both bombed and made little impact on sales.

TOP: This Whistling Billboard is an example of American Flyer's many attempts to reproduce whistle and diesel-horn sounds on a layout. This 577 model, built in 1950, contains a whistle or diesel horn in its base. When a locomotive passes—like the Santa Fe PA in the background—the engineer at the transformer presses a button and the billboard toots or honks.

BOTTOM: The American Flyer Stock Yard vibrated its way into the line in 1950 and stayed there until 1954. After meticulously positioning the Model 736 cattle car into place in front of the cattle chute, a rotary switch started eight little cows furiously vibrating around until—when the chute gate was pushed open with a finger—they filed up the chute and into the stock car. A button push started the vibrating car and also kept the line moving. The instructions suggest, "At times you may find these little critters will get just as stubborn as real cattle and will need a helping hand—just prod them a little and they will continue to move."

other up a ramp and into the waiting car. This turned out to be a very popular accessory. A trick to its success was the application of a dab of Vaseline on each plastic cow so it wouldn't get stuck on the ramp guides and fail to move smoothly into the car.

To complement this gala year, Gilbert commissioned six fifteen-minute films touting the "American Flyer Boys Railroad Club." They were distributed through the Modern Talking Picture Service for showings to groups and for television exposure.

The hefty bill for the 1950 fling came home in the Annual Report of 1951. A.C. explained to grumpy shareholders, "The Santa Fe Streamline Diesel Locomotive [A & B Unit] and extruded aluminum cars, the General Motors Diesel Switcher Locomotive, and the Electronic Whistle; each of these projects necessitated a large capital expenditure and a large increase in manufacturing expenses. All four together put a tremendous burden on our entire staff and financial requirements. The decision to undertake these projects was made in 1949 when sales were tightening up and when competition [Lionel] made it seem an imperative move."

Keeping up with the Joneses was tough for any company that had as many defense contracts as A.C. Gilbert. More than seven million dollars were tied up on its books, all very low profit-margin dollars. The cost of zinc had risen 100 percent, with similar increases in steel, copper, aluminum, and plastics. These price increases had caught Gilbert flat-footed. He continued, "We did not foresee any significant increase ahead in the cost of our materials. . . . What happened . . . showed us the error of these decisions."

The "Nathan Air Chime" whistle was added to the line in 1951 to replace the previous "Electronic Whistle," which had proved erratic in operation. The new "chime" was driven by the transformer rather than by AC power from a wall socket. It was, basically, a tin can containing a vibrator that pushed its sound out through a cardboard speaker. Though ad copy claimed the "air chime" whistle sounded exactly like the real whistle used on more than one hundred American railroads, its actual sound came closer to that made by a small animal caught in a trap.

TOP: Dad must have decided to keep the old car another year in order to afford this American Flyer/Erector spread on the cover of the 1950 Gilbert Toys catalog. No wonder the kids on the stairs are thunderstruck—it must have taken a year of toil to assemble this collection.

BOTTOM: One touch of a button caused the 1955 Model 785 Coal Loader's bucket to descend into a coal bin. A second button closed the bucket and raised it over the internal hopper. Another button push dumped the coal into the hopper, and when enough coal was accumulated for a load, yet another button press emptied the hopper into a car waiting on a parallel track.

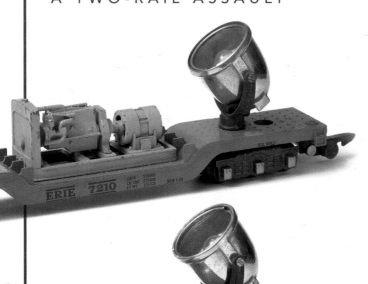

ABOVE: The depressed-center flat car was used for a number of loads, but in 1950 only, it was fitted with a lime-green die-cast generator (top). From 1951 to 1952 American Flyer switched to a dark green plastic generator instead.

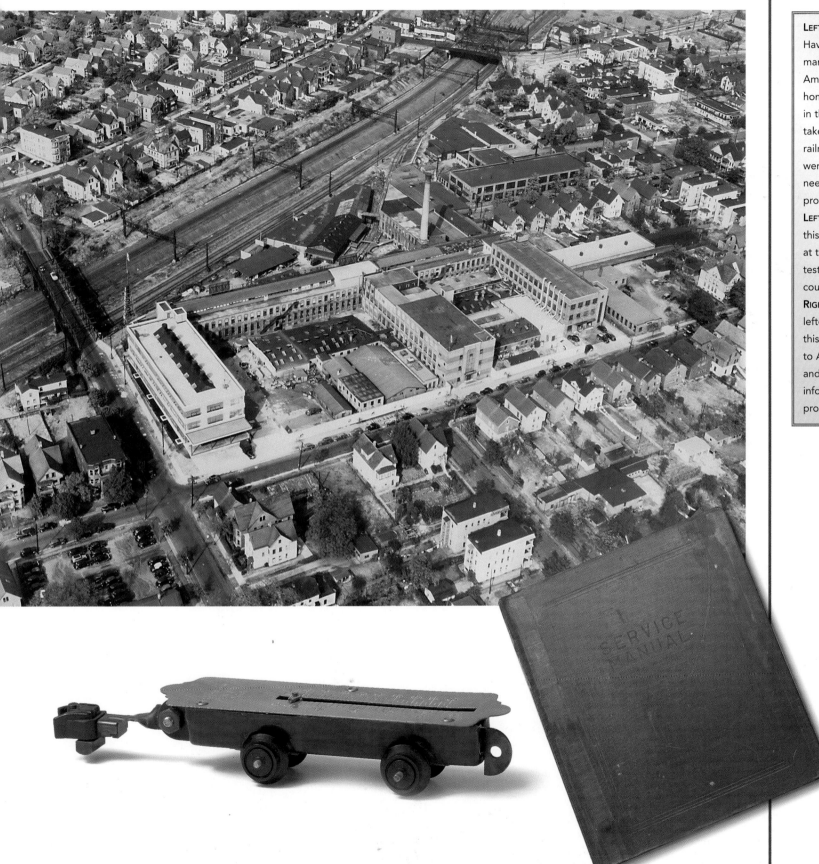

LEFT: The A.C. Gilbert plant in New Haven, Connecticut, was a major manufacturing facility turning out American Flyer trains, Erector sets, home appliances, and other toy lines in the 1950s when this photo was taken. Notice that it also has its own railroad siding. Wings and buildings were added to the basic block as needed by acquisitions and war production.

LEFT BOTTOM: It is speculated that this Gilbert traction device was used at the plant during the 1950s to test locos equipped with knuckle couplers.

RIGHT BOTTOM: Here's another oddity leftover from the 1950s. Most likely, this service manual was shipped out to American Flyer service stations and routinely updated with new information to correspond with new products.

AMERICAN

FLYER

With dealers' shelves and the loading dock still clogged with Circus Train sets, it was cataloged again, but no new sets were made. Compared to the raft of new trains and accessories issued in 1950, 1951 was American Flyer Lite when it came to new products.

Redemption and cost cutting were the touchstones of 1952. Since Lionel had introduced the realistic knuckle coupler in 1945, American Flyer's "realism" claims rang a bit hollow. While A.C. seemed to think the coupler problem was not important—"The older [link] couplers had been efficient and easy"—the engineering staff had been campaigning to produce a knuckle design. Versions of knuckle couplers were studied, but a conservative budget mitigated against a complex design, or retooling the entire line in one swoop. A solid knuckle was proposed and built, but cars could not couple by backing into each other, a prototypical necessity. Scale-size couplers were examined, but were too delicate for rough, tinplate handling. Finally, there were Lionel's patents to avoid. American Flyer didn't need another cease-and-desist letter. Eventually a larger-than-scale design was approved that also circumvented Lionel's patent by having the opening pin move up instead of down to release the knuckle connection.

TOP: An Industrial Brownhoist crane heaves a set of Pike Master trucks from a flat car. Beneath the crane cab, a jack beam can be extended to either side to avoid tipping with heavy loads. This Model 944 is an excellent replica of the real thing. Hand-turned cranks raised and lowered the boom and reeled in the hook, offering exceptional playability back in 1952 when the crane was first offered.

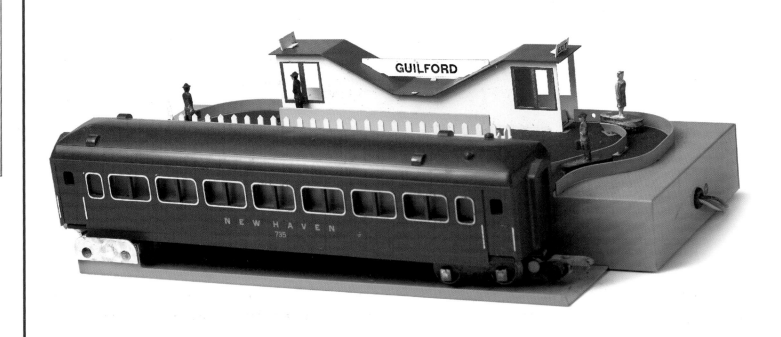

NEW KNUCKLE COUPLERS

Brand new American Flyer Knuckle Couplers that not only operate with 100% efficiency, but LOOK right, too, because they're built to scale. They're not bulky and oversize, but are made to correct freight and passenger car proportions. Built-in hidden coil spring opens knuckle when trip on No. 706 American Flyer remote control Uncoupler or No. 704 manual uncoupler is operated. When one car couples with another, knuckle remains locked in closed position. Two trains in the American Flyer 1952 line, Nos. K5206W and K5210W, (pages 12-13) will be equipped with this new Knuckle Coupler —the BEST OF THEM ALL!

NOTE: Because of emergency conditions beyond our control, The A. C. Gilbert Company reserves the right to change composition, materials, finishes or carton packing, without notice. We cannot guarantee that orders placed will be shipped 100%.

Printed in the U.S.A., Form D 1667A   Copyright 1952. The A. C. Gilbert Company, New Haven, Conn., U.S.A.

In a frugal gesture, these couplers were only offered in two freight sets: one drawn by a Hudson (K5206W) and the other by a Northern (K5210W). Cars sporting the new knuckle couplers were numbered in a 900 series.

Shaving dollars from production costs also caused two locomotives—the C&NW 4-6-2 Pacific and the new 4-4-2 Atlantics—to receive plastic boilers. New plastic tenders were fitted to the Atlantics as well. Plastic also replaced extruded aluminum in the passenger cars attached to the new Silver Streak diesel streamliner. These new lighter-weight cars allowed a full complement of baggage and coach cars to be pulled by the single-motor diesel. No observation car came with the introductory train set. Here again, American Flyer opted for a fictitious train instead of one

with a prototypical railroad name. Even the Santa Fe streamliner became an "American Flyer Lines" team player with its distinctive "Warbonnet" color scheme.

The cost cutters wandering the production floor managed to allow a new feature to the No. 335 Northern Challenger locomotive. By plucking out the turned-brass smokestack and replacing it with an unpainted plastic one, they created "lighted smoke." The engine's headlight in the boiler illuminated the smoke stream from within. The other Flyer locos were spared this so-called feature for the time being.

Finally, in 1953, knuckle couplers spread like a rash through the higher-end American Flyer sets. At the same time, another small, but significant innovation applied rubber tires to the steam engine's drivers. These slip-on tires were called

OPPOSITE BOTTOM: The No. 766 Animated Station Platform and Car was an ingenious addition to the American Flyer accessory line in the early 1950s. The young engineer positioned the special car so a metal finger on the wheel truck came in contact with a strip on the front of the station platform. When the station was activated, four cutout people began vibrating along a chute toward the open car door. When a button was pushed, a vibrating mat in the car began to operate and the people passed into the car. The door at the opposite end of the car was kept shut to keep them inside. To discharge passengers, the second door was opened at the station and the little folk vibrated back out onto the platform.

TOP: Copywriters went a bit overboard when they wrote this blurb for the 1952 introduction of knuckle couplers. "They're not bulky or oversize, but are made to correct freight and passenger car proportions." This was patently not true, but at least Flyer now had parity with Lionel in the coupler wars.

BOTTOM: A.C. Gilbert's coupler evolution for American Flyer trains is summarized here, showing how the smoothly-operating, but unprototypical link coupler evolved from lightweight to weighted versions and then was replaced by the working knuckle coupler. The knuckle went through a few iterations and ended up as the nonworking plastic Pike Master.

Racing past a flagman at trackside, this Model 354 Silver Bullet steam engine picks up speed as it takes us back to 1954. This shrouded Pacific-type 4-6-2 locomotive inherited its lines from the original American Flyer Royal Blue of prewar days. Among the train's features were red glowing smoke, Choo-choo, and a Lucite lens headlight.

AMERICAN

FLYER

"Pul-Mor" and improved traction. Lionel had introduced magnetic rail gripping back in 1950, called Magne-traction. When magnets once again became available as the Korean War ended, this feature received considerable hype. The Flyer solution was both elegant and cheap, if a bit labor intensive.

The Silver Bullet made its debut in 1953. A chromed-up but stripped-down version of the Royal Blue, this Bullet was relegated to the low-end sets and still carried unrealistic link couplers.

Diesel mania produced a collection of the streamliners. The Comet traveled under Missouri Pacific colors, while the Rocket was sort of Rock Island-like in its paint scheme. Even the Santa Fe PA diesel locomotive was revisited, given a third unit that made it an A-B-A, and done up in polished chrome. They were beautiful trains and admirable additions to American Flyer's fleet.

That exceptional GP-7 was reintroduced in dramatic fashion in 1954. In a prototypical coup that left Lionel at the gate, American Flyer rolled out a twin diesel lash-up. A pair of orange-and-black Texas Pacific GP-7s—one powered (No. 375) and a lighted dummy (No. 374)—made their appearance. They were an instant hit. The diesels might have backed down a siding into a Celanese Chemicals tank car that also arrived on the scene that year—if the Flyer fans were quick on their feet. In a burst of chauvinism, A.C. nixed the Celanese advertisement and changed the name on the tanker to "Gilbert Chemicals."

Diesel "Roar," another special-effects noisemaker that simulated either the sound of a diesel engine's rumble or an AM radio station's static, depending on your imagination, was no match for the roar in Gilbert's boardroom as 1955 drew to a close. Through his annual reports, A.C. informed stockholders, "The whole distribution pattern in America is in the throes of a revolution. This revolution manifests itself in the new and enlarged form of 'discount houses' and in rebuttal, dealer price wars. Fair trade, like prohibition, has been proved unenforceable in today's buyers' market. A full-scale attempt to legally enforce price maintenance would bankrupt our company.

"The discounter[s] . . . are cognizant that toys have a very short selling season and legal action takes time as well as money. . . . All this price cutting confusion raises a big question as to how many dealers will be willing to carry and promote our toys . . . or any other product in this class of merchandise."

The flood of American families to the suburbs had propelled the development of farmlands into huge malls—clusters of shops under one roof, anchored by one or two major retailers. Often, these retailers were fast-turnover discount stores, short on staff and long on products with a short shelf life. This new form of merchandising made a huge dent in American Flyer's and Lionel's bottom lines, but had less of an impact on Louis Marx, whose products were geared to quick turnaround, high-volume sales.

Lionel had created a large network of dealerships and good handshake relationships with major department store chains, and was also credited with rescuing the mom-and-pop hardware store from extinction. American Flyer was following the same marketing path. Sears, Wards, Western

TOP: An "air chime" whistle heralded the entry of this Model 477 Alco PA diesel locomotive in its chocolate brown, yellow, orange, and silver (or chrome) livery. The engine was a beauty, especially when lashed to a matching 489 PB unit (which contained the whistle) and a long passenger train. This example wears the softer silver finish offered in 1954.

BOTTOM: This long, sleek model of an Alco PA diesel rolled out of American Flyer shops in 1953 as the Model 466, painted sky blue and yellow with a "Comet" decal (or hot stamping) on its side. The trucks are excellent as are the loco's realistic proportions. The oddity was the nonprototype name and the "American Flyer Lines" logo. Who else ran toy trains on S gauge track? This mysterious marketing spin hung around during the diesel days of the early 1950s.

AMERICAN

FLYER

117

American Flyer Trains
ERECTOR AND OTHER GILBERT TOYS

OPPOSITE: As dawn touches the steel single-track bridge, this 4-8-4 Northern Challenger, built from 1953 to 1956, rolls over a turnout. Additional features such as hand-applied railings, the brass bell, and wire coupler pin lifters gave the scale model its "railroady" look.

TOP: By the time this 1953 catalog was in the hands of youngsters, knuckle couplers had spread throughout the line. The Comet and Rocket diesels were hauling passenger sets up and down the pages. The Gilbert Hall of Science was going full steam and American Flyer was riding high.

Tire and Auto—all the major chains offered at least some Flyer sets and demonstration layouts. Lionel had been cultivating its customer base since World War I, whereas American Flyer in New Haven had been at it for only about ten years. Flyer had a much steeper learning curve, despite the carryover of salespeople from the Chicago American Flyer staff.

Another factor eroding toy train sales was the decline of America's railroads, as airlines and long-haul trucking undermined rail transport. President Eisenhower had created a national network of interstate highways "to aid national defense and the movement of troops and materiel," said the administration at every opportunity. Trucking companies, the people who built trucks, and the oil industry all flourished. Airlines faced little regulation as airports grew, aviation-fuel sales tripled, and large tracts of land near metropolitan

centers quadrupled in value, as airlines were courted by state and local politicians.

What the railroads got was a thick book of regulations, enforced by the Interstate Commerce Commission, outlining with whom, what, and where the railroads could do business. Part of this regulatory nightmare could be laid at the railroads' own doorstep, a retribution of sorts for the railroads' behavior when they were the only game in town. Shippers had paid the railroads steep rates, and the construction and maintenance of ornate passenger terminals were part of the going price to keep trains servicing a community. While many of the railroads' extortion was well remembered, what was forgotten were the sacrifices made during World War II. Unlike World War I, the railroads had remained under independent operation during the war and had more than fulfilled the country's desperate need for goods and

AMERICAN

FLYER

troop transportation. Rail traffic had transported 90 percent of all goods and 75 percent of all passenger traffic during the conflict. They deserved better than they got in the 1950s (and beyond).

The fate of the red ink–bleeding railroads directly affected the toy train industry. As the railroads were perceived to be less relevant to American life, kids' attention gravitated to new toys. Cold War politicians were fighting the "godless" communists hiding behind every bush. Rockets were arcing across every military test range. Cracks were appearing in stucco homes near Nevada's bomb-testing sites. Television brought all this activity into almost everyone's home as a forest of antennas sprouted on America's rooftops. Toy companies knew how to exploit television with kid shows built around new products. But even though Lionel and American Flyer tried their hand at television exploitation, their efforts never made a substantial impact on the bottom line. Interest in toy trains was beginning to flag.

The A.C. Gilbert Company was more fortunate than Lionel, since Gilbert had always maintained a toy line and a popular line of home appliances. What was beginning to happen, however, was that the profits from Gilbert's other businesses were being offset by American Flyer losses. Lionel and American Flyer were feeling the pressure of changing times and, for both toy train companies, everything came to a head in 1959.

Left: A chubby Atlantic 4-4-2 rolls out of a tunnel in 1954. Of all the locomotives built by American Flyer, Atlantics—varying sharply in quality from 1938 to the late 1960s—were the most numerous. With its fat O gauge boiler and large Wootten-type fire box, the S gauge Flyer Atlantic was far from graceful, but it was surely the most ubiquitous steamer in the line.

Top: A tale of two gauges is told here—featuring the B&O 980 boxcar offered between 1956 and 1957. In S gauge, the No. 980 boxcar is a painted model over a black plastic shell. Next to it is its Gilbert 33513 HO counterpart. Production on these sets continued up to 1963. During the 1950s, many S gauge cars were duplicated in HO gauge.

AMERICAN

FLYER

TOP: Simply called the No. 586 Wayside Station, this rural platform added a nice touch to passenger yards from 1946 to 1956. The set came with people and handcarts.
BOTTOM: Illustrations from American Flyer's 1957 catalog cover feature a striking diesel set running an Alco PA at the head end of a Northern Pacific passenger set. For maximum realism, this unique set uses the Northern Pacific logo and paint scheme in place of the usual American Flyer logo.

All Cars Accurately Scaled from Northern Pacific R. R. Blueprints!

TOP: Gliding into a turn, this Model 492 Alco PA in Northern Pacific livery shows off its Far Eastern–inspired yin-and-yang logo on its head end. Silver die-cast trucks revealed exquisite detail, and a full operating knuckle coupler is mounted to the four-wheel truck for some flexibility of operation in the passenger yard.

LEFT BOTTOM: This illustration shows the drumhead rear end of the Northern Pacific observation car and the vistadome car in detail.

RIGHT BOTTOM: Check out the little man operating the Model 787 Log Loader, a 1955 reissue of the 1946 original accessory. Logs are picked up from the inclined ramp by wire hooks and dropped onto the waiting car. Action happens as long as the button is held down. A No. 914 log dump car from 1953 that's parked in front can later redeposit the logs to start the cycle all over again.

TOP: As the sun sets, the passengers in this 1953 Hamilton vistadome car enjoy a friendly cocktail as their train glides through the mountains. Vista-domes were popular with cross-country travelers and became big selling points as the railroads struggled to improve their postwar revenue flow. American Flyer made sure they offered vista-dome cars on most of their sets to follow the trend.

LEFT BOTTOM: The Model 936 flat car was built in 1948. The depressed-center flat car with its wire-spool load is lettered for the Erie Railroad. The cable is, apparently, destined for the "American Flyer Lines" plant in New Haven. The heavy-duty hauler rolls on realistic six-wheel trucks and has link couplers.

RIGHT BOTTOM: This Tuscan-red Grand Canyon observation car from 1956 had a "brakeman" who leaned out whenever the car stopped and the current was broken. A solenoid mechanism returned him to the platform when the car started up again. This No. 978 used the same mechanism as the No. 977 Caboose. The wraparound rear gating has been cut away to allow for the figure's movement.

OPPOSITE: Revealed in its full length, the 4-8-4 Northern-type American Flyer locomotive demonstrates its scale proportions and detail. With its signature white tires, action valve gear, and excellent casting, the engine was a standout model. With smoke billowing and Choo-choo grinding away, this steamer was the high watermark of Flyer design and engineering.

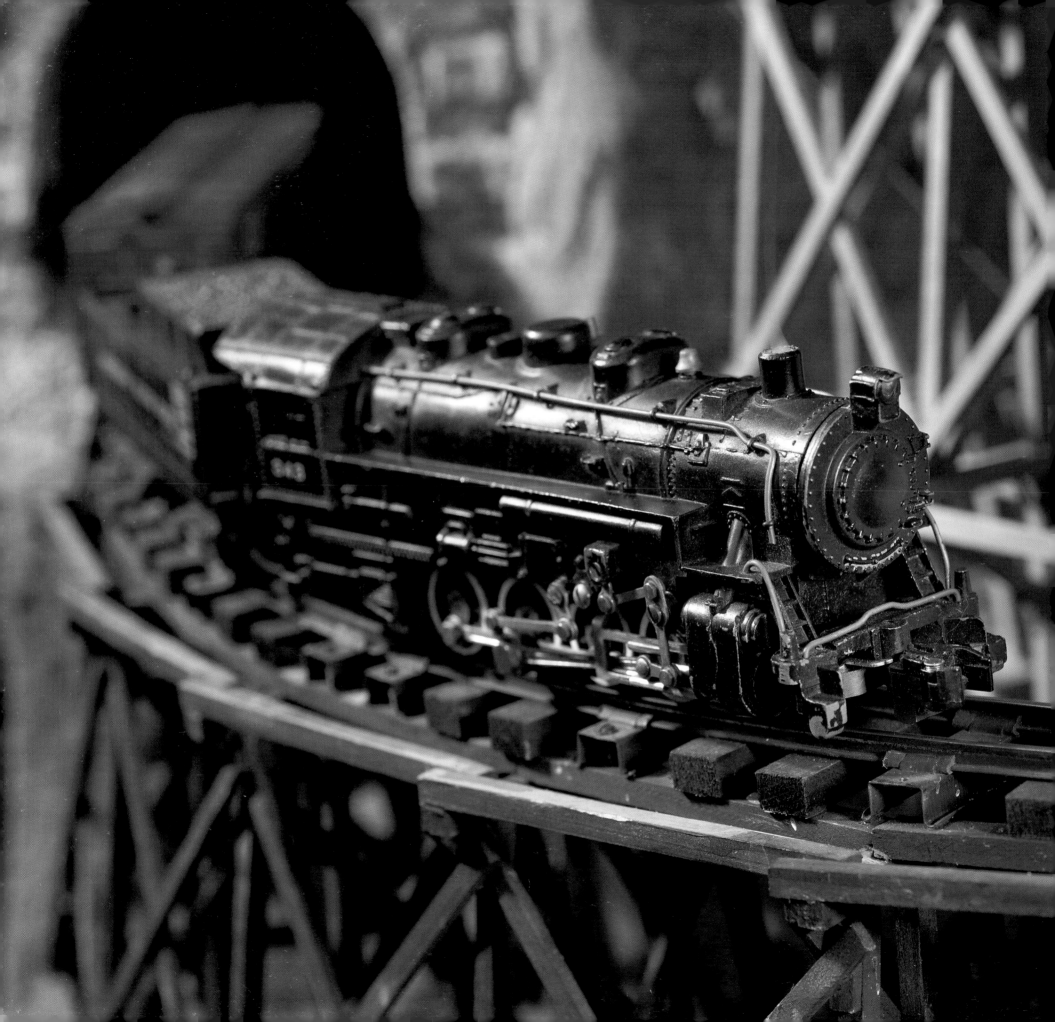

OPPOSITE: Always on the look-out for a unique prototype, American Flyer debuted the Model 343 0-8-0 switcher in O gauge in 1941, and brought it back to the tracks as an S gauge loco (pictured) in 1946. The 0-8-0 was modeled after a nickel plate prototype that was a heavy-duty yard goat. This 343 version, built from 1953 to 1956, had all the goodies from smoke and Choo-choo to Pull-Mor tires on those drive wheels for extra hauling power.

LEFT TOP: In 1949, this Model 760 Automatic Highway Flasher was added to many rug railroads. Wired to a clip placed farther up the track, this crossing guard flashes its lights as a train passes.

RIGHT TOP: A Model 740 handcar hauls three tipple cars from a mine passage as part of the 5300T Miners Work Train set offered between 1953 and 1954. The handcar did not normally haul rolling stock, but had a drawbar added to its frame with this set that accepted the tipple cars' couplers. Normally, this little action car zipped around the layout with its two track workers pumping like mad. The Model 742 added a reverse unit that was activated whenever the handcar hit something.

BOTTOM: Union Station, Model 793, designed to represent a concrete passenger station, was fully illuminated inside—as seen through these eleven (of fourteen total) windows. Designed in 1954, the station added an urban touch to any layout.

AMERICAN

FLYER

LEFT TOP: The last of the whistling billboards came out in plastic in 1956, ending a long line of tooting signs that added railroad sounds to a layout without tripping over Lionel's patented whistle system. Eventually, American Flyer solved the whistle problem and the billboards became superfluous.

RIGHT TOP: Sitting poised for launch from the pedestal on its flat car, this missile from 1957 marks an attempt by American Flyer to be relevant to Cold War culture. This No. 969 launch pad is operated by a solenoid that releases a pin, thereby sending the rocket skyward, powered by a compressed spring. The rocket could also travel as cargo locked in the white bracket.

BOTTOM: Distinctive in its black, red, and white livery, the Model 497 New Haven diesel, built in 1957, was powered by one double worm drive motor. Its roofline was studded with ventilators, a horn, and other cast-on details that were typical of the American Flyer diesel fleet.

TOP: Dating back to 1938, the A.C. Gilbert American Flyer floodlight car idea was modified over the years and was always a popular addition to a night freight. Originally offered in stamped steel, the concept was modified until this example, the Model 934, was rolled out in 1954. An aluminum-finished lamp housing directs the beam upward. With a die-cast frame and knuckle couplers, the floodlight car had many hand-applied details and looked best hooked up to a work train.

BOTTOM: The Missouri Pacific passenger set (Mo-Pac Flier) clears a bridge over a gorge. Considered by many to be *the* most desirable passenger set issued by American Flyer, this 1958 string of silver, blue, and yellow cars looks great behind its Alco PA diesel loco. Shown here are the Eagle Valley observation car, the Eagle Lake coach, and the Eagle Creek vistadome car.

TOP: The end of the 1958 Missouri Valley observation car shows the die-cast details and the (unfortunate) paper sticker where an illuminated drumhead should have been.

BOTTOM: Introduced in 1955, this 1957 version of the 797 bay window caboose has a conductor or brakeman standing on the rear platform looking out at the train. Press the button and he pops back out of sight. Release the button and he resumes his vigil.

LEFT: This 21004 0-6-0 switcher from 1957 waits patiently on a siding. The switcher, made of black plastic, has both Choo-choo and smoke capabilities. While the tender is lettered "American Flyer Lines," a Pennsylvania Railroad keystone is stamped just below the coal bin. Good-looking side rods and realistic crosshead action added to its semi-scale appearance, making this model of the Pennsy B-6 prototype very popular.

AMERICAN

FLYER

CHAPTER SIX

THE NAME CARRIES ON

This Year, 1959, marks the Golden Anniversary of the A.C. Gilbert Company. Just fifty years ago A.C. Gilbert, newly graduated from Yale's Medical School and holding an Olympic Pole Vaulting Championship, established a small magic manufacturing business in Westville [Gilbert's original location], Connecticut, a suburb of New Haven. Half a century later the business was to become one of the largest toy companies in the world and the leader in producing science sets and electric trains.

So proclaimed the 1959 American Flyer catalog, which then went on to defend the company's trimming the line of trains to nine sets from eighteen sets in 1958. "The Most Compact Train Line in American Flyer History!" boomed a headline. Even though the line had been pruned, some new additions were tested in an attempt to find that magic product that would reverse the company's downward trend.

A Baldwin diesel switcher (No. 21812) had been painted with Texas Pacific colors and hooked onto the "Rambler" freight set. A double-ended New Haven EP-5 electric (No. 21573) had been added to the lineup and now ran with a set of passenger cars bearing orange stripes. There were new paint schemes, such as the yellow safety stripes slapped on the little 21156 Docksider 0-6-0, but at the cost of the loco's Choo-choo and smoke features.

An attempt was made to burnish the anniversary event. Maury Romer, ever the enthusiastic believer, tried an idea that had brought attention to American Flyer when it was still in Chicago. He suggested a gold-plated train. Harking back to the cadmium-plated Mayflower

PREVIOUS PAGES: A Gilbert twelve-wheel DL-600 Alco diesel in HO gauge climbs through a turn in C&O livery. The HO line went bust again in the 1960s and was resurrected by General Mills Fundimensions/MPC Group in 1970—only to peter out for good in 1977.

BOTTOM: Heading up the 1959 push was the much ballyhooed Frontiersman train set. This Civil War–period loco and cars tagged onto the recent glut of Western shows on television and in the movies. This catalog marked the golden anniversary of the A.C. Gilbert Company.

OPPOSITE: Westerns and the Civil War were hot TV and movie themes in the late 1950s. Both Lionel and American Flyer created 4-4-0 American-type diamond and funnel-stack wood-burning locomotives—complete with passenger and freight car sets—in 1959. The 21088 Franklin was American Flyer's entry. Garishly colored and simplistic in detailing, the engine was loaded with smoke, reverse unit, and Pull-Mor tires on the rear driver pair.

Wide gauge train from the late 1920s, he used Gilbert's vacuum-metalizing process, which was capable of putting a gold finish on plastic, and turned out six gleaming passenger sets. They were sent to the Gilbert Halls of Science.

The gold-plated curiosity sets achieved the same success as Chicago Flyer's Mayflower trains had thirty years earlier. They were big duds.

A.C. Gilbert chose that year to retire from active participation in the company. He had brought his son, A.C. Gilbert Jr.— called "Al"—into the company. Al Jr. abandoned his profession as an electrical engineer and climbed up through the company hierarchy to the office of president. A.C. had been slowing down over the last couple of years and figured Al could finally take over the reins. Though A.C. continued to attend meetings, his son was in charge.

Stockholders were told in the 1959 Annual Report: "In general, consumer demand is

for low-priced trains in the $19.95 to $39.95 range and, consequently, our product development program is putting continual emphasis on offering sets at a lower price." They concluded by projecting that all that was needed was increased advertising, packaging, and display schemes to pump up the "American Flyer S gauge" trains.

By now, Gilbert American Flyer was committed to the same marketing strategy the company had identified as a reason Chicago American Flyer had failed: selling for price only to reduce the profit drag on other businesses.

Searching for answers, Al brought in the firm of Booz, Allen & Hamilton to make recommendations. The authors of the consulting firm's study put the burden on sales and engineering departments that they deemed "not aggressive enough." New people were brought in, other people were shuffled around, and sales policies were appropriately modified. One of those policies was the sweeping closure of all the Halls of Science.

The consultants' report claimed that toy salespeople came into New York, stopped at the toy manufacturers' centers at 200 Fifth Avenue and 1107 Broadway, and then blew out of town without giving Gilbert's Hall of Science a glance. Gilbert's salespeople objected to the closings, saying Lionel, their biggest competitor, was even farther away from the toy manufacturers' centers.

They were right. The buyers weren't stopping at Lionel either. Sales numbers were grim over there as well. Joshua Cowen had lost interest in his company, as toy trains faded from kids' wish lists. He was getting old and tired, and had groomed his son, Lawrence, to take over.

More aggressive product development was also on the consultants' to-do list. Television was cranking out westerns at this time and American Flyer grabbed at that brass ring. Following a big teaser ad campaign, the Frontiersman Civil War period locomotive and passenger set was trumpeted. Also referred to as the Franklin passenger set and the Overland Express, after the name on the cars, the set was headed by a 4-4-0 American-type, funnel-stack locomotive. A new numbering system logged the set as No. 20550. The set was modeled after a kit-bash created from an

TOP: An HO version of the S gauge Frontiersman train was created in 1959 to help herald the manufacturer's fiftieth anniversary, but Gilbert didn't build it. The Mantua-Tyco Company of Woodbury Heights, New Jersey, which had been making passenger coaches for Gilbert's HO line, trotted out an existing 1860s vintage train. The Mantua General locomotive was transformed into the Frontiersman with a new paint job and decals. Because of the HO locomotive's slender boiler, the DC motor powering the drive via a flexible cable was located in the tender. Once boxed by Gilbert at the New Haven plant, the train set consisting of the loco, tender, combine, and coach, became set No. 35099 and sold for $29.98 without track or power pack. The sets were discontinued in 1960.

BOTTOM: The Civil War–inspired train set did not help Gilbert's bottom line. In various liveries, the locomotive and tender still exist today with the motor in the tender connected to the drive wheels by a flexible cable.

OPPOSITE: Overland Express cars were built to follow the Franklin Civil War–period steam engine built between 1959 and 1961. This baggage car is plastic with simulated wood sides. The "FY & P" stands for "Fifty Years and Progress," since this Frontiersman set was brought out in 1959. You can see the truss rods under the body and the operating knuckle couplers.

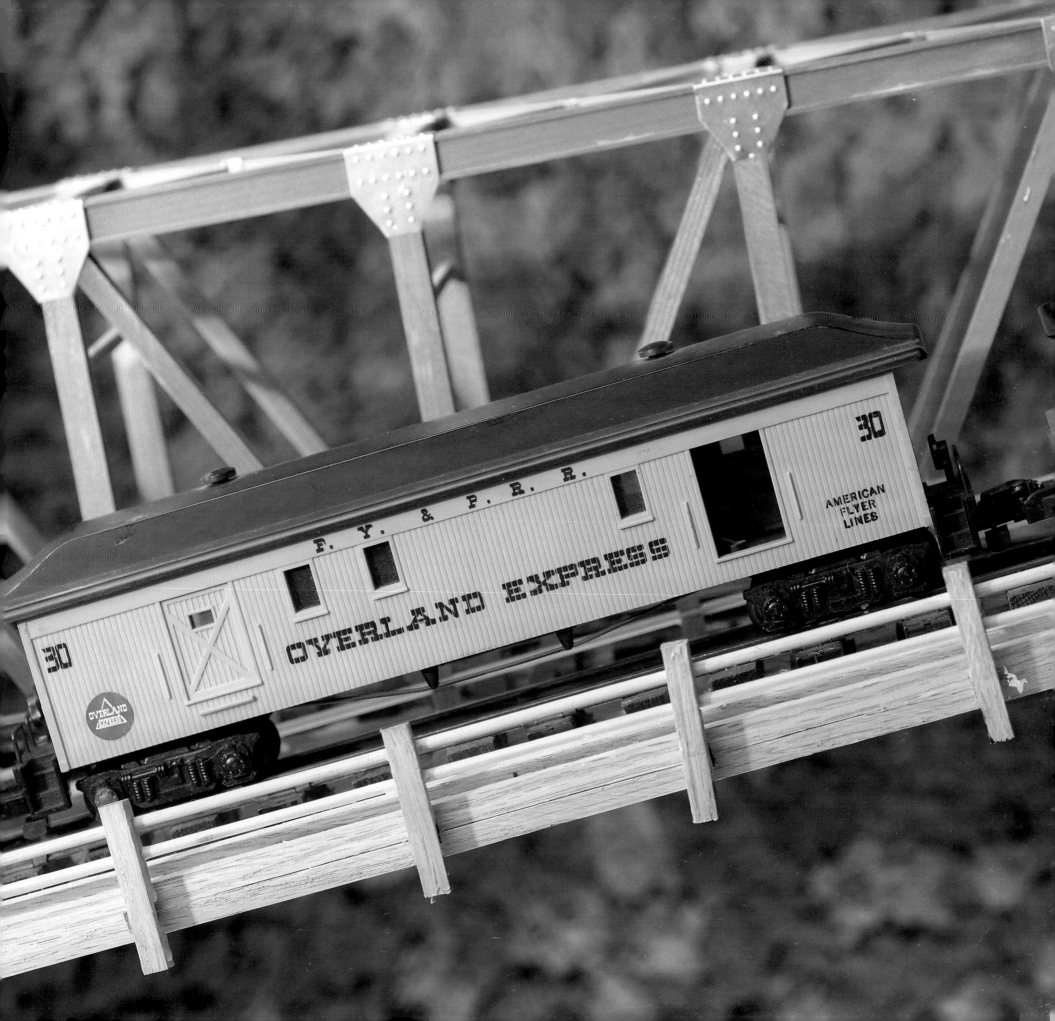

anniversary was "Fifty Years and Progress," the railroad name became the F.Y.&P.R.R.

According to Maury Romer, sales engineer for American Flyer, news of the Frontiersman broke at a hobby show in January, giving Lionel a couple of months to cobble together its own Civil War train in time for the New York Toy Fair in March. Whatever happened, Lionel put out its General Civil War period train set on the cover of its 1959 catalog. Sharing the cover with this Civil War vintage train, in a blaze of anachronistic overkill, were missile-firing cars, ICBMs blasting off from gantries, and the dogged old Berkshire steam engine. Clearly, Lionel was also searching for a handle on the market.

Flyer officials blamed market saturation of old-time trains for the Frontiersman's poor sales. If American Flyer had been running on three-rail track, saturation could have been a factor, but the quality of the set was largely to blame as far as two-rail fans were concerned. Originally, the cars were painted yellow, but they were then made of yellow plastic to reduce paint costs. Red trim on the locomotive

American Flyer Atlantic motor and chassis, surrounded by a wood-burner boiler, funnel stack, high drivers, and cowcatcher. A museum owner and custom loco builder in Yardley, Pennsylvania, sold the model to Flyer. It became the template for the new Frontiersman. While it was being constructed for the 1959 golden anniversary release, the toy train's designers realized that the yellow open-end coaches making up the passenger train needed a railroad name above the windows. Since the slogan for the was also shifted from painted plastic to colored plastic. The catalog for consumers had been reduced to a single, folded sheet printed in color, while the dealers' catalog had color only on the cover.

As skids of unsold Frontiersman trains backed up in the shipping department, Gilbert began to seek ways to unload the sets. The Truscott Company came up with a plan to do just that. This outfit had saved Kodak's bacon when the photography giant had been stuck with a dud camera. Using advertising and promotional gimmicks, Truscott had cleared out Kodak's inventory. Truscott proposed packaging the Frontiersman set with a bag of plastic cowboys and American Indians and frontier scenery, together with a Kodak camera and a roll of film. The little tyke was supposed to set up the train, the cowboys, and the scenery, then photograph the result. Gilbert took the bait, and carloads of these packages were shipped to Chicago, along with considerable hoopla.

On arrival in Chicago, the entire shipment was impounded by the sheriff. Chicago-based *Encyclopedia Britannica* had been laying in wait for Truscott, in order to collect monies the company owed *Brittanica* for a failed promotional deal. American Flyer took a $380,000 bath and A.C. Gilbert posted an $80,000 loss.

By now, American Flyer was in full retreat. In 1960, automatic knuckle couplers were replaced by solid dummy couplers on many cars and coal tenders. Operating cars included the 25046 Rocket Launcher flat car and the exploding 25057 TNT box car. Cost cutting was apparent in the Chief passenger train set, headed up by a single-motor 21927 Santa Fe PA locomotive. Rivets now held the cars together instead of screws, and the drumhead on the rear of the observation car was a paper sticker rather than the illuminated version. Virtually all metal frames were gone, replaced by plastic. Some accessories touted in the catalog, such as the 23320 Traffic Master, were never produced.

On January 24, 1961, A.C. Gilbert died at the New England Baptist Hospital of a lingering heart problem that had kept him there for several weeks. The sorrow that sucked the life out of the company seemed to be reflected in the products of 1961, and those pushed out the door in

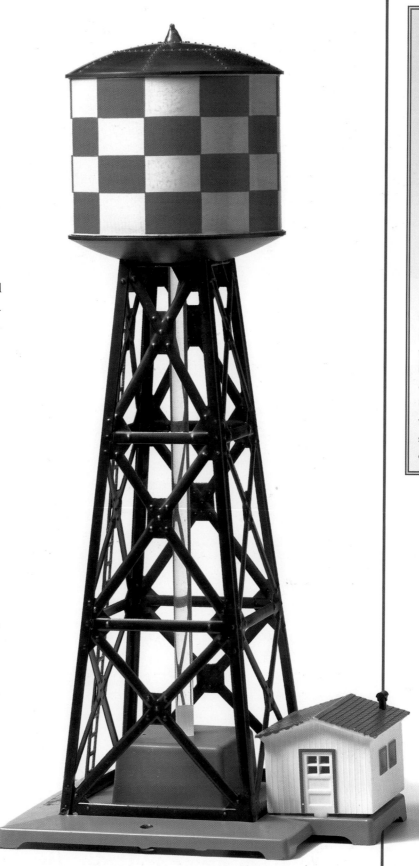

OPPOSITE TOP: The head-on view of the 22256 Docksider of 1959 shows clearly the water saddle tank that was draped over the boiler. The Docksider—unique to the Baltimore & Ohio Railroad—carried its own coal as well. This later American Flyer version had front and rear knuckle couplers and Pull-Mor rubber tires, but only two electrical pickups.

OPPOSITE BOTTOM: The Frontiersman train lasted from 1959 to 1960, but its execution was less than the promotional hype. It was built in S gauge and HO gauge—and neither one was a big hit.

LEFT: This 23772 Bubbling Tower was the same as the 772 Tower except for the checkerboard red white tank. When powered up, a bulb in the base heats a transparent oil-base goo that begins to bubble. Unfortunately, the clear goo sometimes overheated and became a solid mess. This model was cataloged from 1957 to 1964.

AMERICAN

FLYER

American Flyer's few remaining years. Gilbert had been the soul of his company, a towering presence offering assurance that a steady hand was always on the throttle.

A.C.'s son, Al, was more of a consensus manager. He brought in people to help him steer the company. For that year's Annual Report, he wrote, "1961 was not one of our more notable years from the standpoint of sales volume and profits. . . . The decline in sales last year . . . can in great part be attributed to the lessening interest in electric trains by today's youngsters."

The most interesting part of that report's outlook was his closing line: "By far the biggest news of all, and a major milestone in the 52 year history of your company has been our new association with the Wrather Corporation of California." Except for a parenthetical reference to the date

TOP: The Cow on the Track accessory was silly, but fun. The unit was placed next to an electrically isolated section of track. Pressing a red button moved the cow on the track which caused the loco to stop automatically. Press a green button, the cow moves out of the way and the train proceeds. The whoops of laughter lasted from 1957 to 1959.
BOTTOM: Keeping with the theme that toys that go "Boom!" are popular, American Flyer built this Model 25057 TNT box car. Press a button and the five-piece plastic shell flies into pieces.

TOP: A little blue 0-6-0 Docksider loco rolled into the yard in 1959. When first introduced in 1958 as the 21155, the model offered a full range of features including smoke, Choo-choo sounds, working knuckle couplers, Pull-Mor rubber tires on its drive wheels, and four electric contact pick-up shoes. A year later, this 21158 was shipped out with fixed (dummy) knuckle couplers, no reverse unit (which makes car switching in a yard quite tough), and only two pick-up shoes (which caused sporadic stops and starts).

BOTTOM: This 23796 Sawmill from 1957 is a hoot to watch. The illusion offered is that the log in the sliding log holder passes by the whirling plastic saw blade and lops off pieces of the log to turn them into boards. These are, in turn, plucked from the stack of boards in the sawmill house by a little man riding in a boom chair, and then loaded into a slot at the top of the house. Couple this accessory with the 23787 Log Loader and a logging industry is created.

TOP: Shipped out in 1960, this Baker's Chocolate tank car, Model 24330, is an example of the gradual dumbing-down, or as AF claimed, "more efficiently produced" rolling stock. The tank is white plastic with handrails that no longer extend around the ends. The tank is held to the frame with one screw, and solid Pike Master couplers are on each end. Still, it's a good-looking car of accurate proportions.

BOTTOM: This very credible work caboose saw the end of its production run in 1964. A pair of Pike Master solid couplers are installed fore and aft, denoting this model as one of the last of its line.

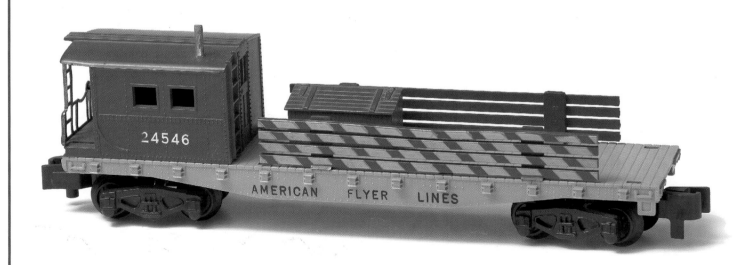

TOP: Dating from the downside years of American Flyer, this red, unpainted-plastic body and plastic load of gravel arrived between 1960 and 1965. It could be found with either operating knuckle couplers (early) or Pike Master dummy couplers (late). This model has operating couplers.

LEFT BOTTOM: Trains have become just another part of Gilbert's "World of Transportation" as airplanes and "Auto-Rama" race cars jockey for discount store shelf space in the 1960s.

RIGHT BOTTOM: This U.S.A.F. Rocket sled was built in Flyer's declining days between 1960 and 1964, giving kids something to speed around the layout.

AMERICAN

FLYER

of his death in the list of directors, A.C. Gilbert's name was not mentioned in the Annual Report at all.

Al Jr. was concerned because the Gilbert family owned 51 percent of the company's stock. The loss of his father at the helm was an obvious blow to the company's perceived stability. He needed to protect that investment and shore up confidence of other shareholders so he called in the Wrather Corporation, which was interested in adding a toy business to its wide range of holdings.

Jack Wrather had created a company that built pleasure boats, owned the Muzak Company that piped music into corporate facilities, and produced the television programs *Lassie* and *The Royal Mounties*, two highly rated kids' programs. He was a pioneer in creating a "conglomerate" of companies under a single corporate umbrella, a trend that flowered later in the 1960s. He came into the A.C. Gilbert Company as chairman in 1962, together with William Quinlan Jr. Al Gilbert remained on board as president.

The big train introduced in 1961 was the F9 diesel locomotive. This tragic little pug-nosed plastic diesel was the cheapest possible "toy" train American Flyer could produce. The public viewed it as a cheap Lionel knockoff: too high and too short. Its one big feature was a working headlight. One not half-bad idea was "Pike Master" track with lots of plastic ties that looked prototypical and allowed a tighter operating radius. To operate on this track, locomotives like the venerable GP-7 had their steps trimmed off so their trucks could follow the track curve.

As Wrather's people were moving into their offices at the New Haven plant, American Flyer cut its "Most Compact Line" from nine train sets down to six. They all came with Pike Master track and one old veteran made its last appearance. The New York Central Hudson showed up with a permanently attached tender and a full complement of Pull-Mor tires, Choo-choo, smoke, and remote-control reverse. In its freight consist came the No. 25062 Exploding Mine Car. Press a button and "Boom!" it explodes. The arrival of this set was like a runner who makes one last sprint before collapsing across the finish line.

In 1963 A.C. Gilbert Jr. died suddenly of a brain tumor and the Wrather Company assumed full corporate control.

Besides tearing out all the piped-in music Gilbert had installed and replacing it with Muzak, the Wrather people began thrashing around, searching for stunning toy ideas. American Flyer trains were demoted to the bottom of the A.C. Gilbert line.

As Gilbert toys such as the "Winged Thing" and "Scrubble Bubble" descended on an unsuspecting public, the all-time classic Gilbert Erector Set got a makeover, which redesigned its basic parts and included lots of plastic elements. Longtime A.C. Gilbert veterans almost wept at the sacrilege. The big train for 1964 was the Casey Jones, a 4-4-0 with Burlington logo variations on the tender. At best, this was a stunted twig on American Flyer's illustrious family tree. It was the steam engine equivalent of the pale, squeezed F9 diesel. The locomotive's side rods were minimal, window "reflections" were dabbed in the opaque cab window frames. The clunky-looking steamers pulled little freight sets.

Once-sleek passenger trains had dwindled down to a single set trimmed in plastic, the four-car Missouri Pacific Eagle, pulled by a 21920 Alco PA. The riveted plastic cars made up the last A.C. Gilbert American Flyer passenger train set. Still rolling along among these lame last gasps of a once-great line of elegant scale-model trains was the old Hudson, towing an eight-car freight, the No. 20768 Smoky Mountain set. The locomotive type that was proudly modeled by Chicago American Flyer back in 1936 was there at the end.

Desperately casting around for some gimmick to turn the train line's fortunes around, the company came up with a "Game Train," using a Casey Jones 4-4-0 loco, three cars, a circle of track, and a game board with pieces that allowed three different games to be played. While this idea laid a giant egg, the "board" concept raised somebody's consciousness. In 1965, the "All Aboard" idea was launched with a full-color catalog and much drum beating.

You could assemble an "All Aboard" layout complete with roads, trees, tunnels, and other scenery by purchasing interlocking panels that connected neatly together. For example, the Champion 800 set had eight panels with full scenic details, track, and two remote-control switches. A 4-4-2 Pennsylvania Railroad, Atlantic-type loco hauled a four-car freight around the pre-laid Pike Master track. If you

OPPOSITE: This HO gauge 32404 caboose waits on a cold and lonely siding. Sold for two dollars ready-to-run, the little die-cast cabin car looked good and was simple to manufacture with its one-piece brass platform stampings. Success in the HO line was not to be. HO sales volumes in the 1960s favored smaller, less-capitalized companies.

TOP: These motorized units were designed to just zip around the track. Most were built in the early 1950s, but this particular model arrived between 1960 and 1964. It is the more common version; by comparison the "743" maintenance car is quite rare. Both are powered by a cheap Japanese-built motor.

AMERICAN

FLYER

GILBERT

CAREER BUILDING
SCIENCE TOYS

The A. C. Gilbert Company • Erector Square • New Ha...

ERECTOR

1962

had greater ambitions, there was the Western 1200 set, consisting of twelve panels. This set included fancy frills, such as a track crossing, and a whistle hidden in a house, rather than a billboard. A No. 21085 Milwaukee K-5 Pacific towed a five-car freight through the scenery.

To expand a layout, extra panels could be bought and track plans were available for a number of configurations. Holes were drilled in the plastic base for the addition of signs, billboards, trees, and other scenery elements that could be purchased separately. The well-known Marvin Glass Company, a toy design shop in Chicago, created the panels and had them hand-painted in Portugal. Glass' services didn't come cheap, however; the potentially good idea was undercut by packaging a cheap-looking train set with the panels. A number of separate cars were offered, including a No. 24533 track-cleaning car for the Pike Master track. Some

people ripped up the Pike Master and replaced it with regular Flyer two-rail tinplate track if the curves' radii weren't too tight. Despite its initial promise, the All Aboard layout system became, as Maury Romer recalls, "one of the better-known flops in the toy train business."

The catalog for 1965 contained a mere fourteen items. In 1966, they sprinkled artificial snow on All Aboard panels and called the set "Winter Wonderland." Except for a few desultory rolling stock odds and ends, that was it.

A new president, Anson Isaacson, was brought in to lead the A.C. Gilbert Company and he, in turn, signed on a number of people from the Ideal Toy Company, his former place of employment. It was this high-salaried entourage that shouldered American Flyer into the warehouses. Isaacson was chauffeured back and forth from his home in New York to New Haven on the A.C. Gilbert Company's tab. His mandate was to eliminate all individual rolling stock and locomotive sales, and incorporate everything into train sets. Employees worked long hours before Christmas to make up train sets from individually boxed inventory. At the end of the big push, time cards were put in a box for a drawing. The winner got a Mustang automobile, the runner-up walked away with a color television set, and the third-place prize was a hi-fi set.

More product was created than could ever be sold. What was left of American Flyer's 1966 offerings filled a warehouse that was sold to the Westminster Products Company, the company that once provided the sales-incentive premiums and giveaways for Gilbert. The Wrather Corporation began looking for a buyer for what remained of the A.C. Gilbert Company.

On September 8, 1965, Joshua Lionel Cowen died of a heart attack in Palm Beach, Florida. Unlike A.C. Gilbert, Cowen had lived just long enough to see Lionel, the company he had built, slide into ruin. Cowen had placed his son, Lawrence, in charge. Like Al Jr., Lawrence wasn't quite up to the task. While Lawrence was still president, Joshua and the rest of the family sold their shares to a group headed up by Roy Marcus Cohn, Cowen's great nephew. Roy Cohn had made his name working for Senator Joseph McCarthy during

the infamous Army-McCarthy hearings in the mid-1950s. The communist witch-hunt had ruined McCarthy, but Cohn survived to practice law in New York. He was also a promoter and free-spending entrepreneur. As soon as he and his group took over Lionel, he went on a spending spree, accumulating a number of companies that had nothing to do with toy trains.

When Cohn finally skipped out of Lionel, two jumps ahead of a process server trying to impound Cohn's limousine for back debts, Lionel was a Gordian knot of interlocking companies, all of which were losing money.

In 1967, Joshua Cowen's son, Lawrence, died of a heart attack and Lionel bought the American Flyer name and what toy train bits and pieces were left from Wrather for $150,000. The name that had survived sixty years of competition was added to the flotsam floating atop Lionel's sea of red ink.

The great rivalry continued to link the names American Flyer and Lionel, even after they had exhausted themselves in a changed world. Lionel was eventually bought up by General Mills, as the "conglomerate" era rolled into the 1970s. General Mills licensed the use of the Lionel name for a royalty paid to Ronald Saypol, Cowen's grandson-in-law and Lionel's last president. Along with the Lionel name, General Mills inherited American Flyer as well.

From one regime to the next that bought the Lionel name and assets, American Flyer has gone along for the ride, from General Mills' "Fundimensions" division, which discovered that Lionel collectors comprised a real and viable market, to Richard Kughn's time at the throttle, beginning in 1987. Kughn raised the Lionel name to its previous place of dominance in the toy train market, then sold out to the Wellspring Group—an investment organization that specializes in turning around low-profit companies—which took over in 1993. For the time being, a few American Flyer diesels and bits of rolling stock can still be found in the back of a Lionel catalog.

American Flyer's O gauge and two-rail, S gauge trains take their well-deserved place alongside Lionel just as the dedicated group of Flyer collectors and operators that soldier on today still form a loyal following in the toy train world. American Flyers were wonderful trains in their respective

Created by Fundimensions out of Lionel in 1981, this American Flyer powerhouse mounts two double worm drive motors in back-to-back (A-A) Alco PAs in Southern Pacific livery. The Model 8150 had all eight wheels powered in each unit, and all had traction tires. As a hauler of streamlined passenger cars, this combo unit had the muscle to pull nails out of a wall.

AMERICAN

FLYER

JAMES BOND 007 ROAD RACE
LE MANS START

JUMP METER

GILBERT AMERICAN FLYER
All Aboard

ALL LANDSCAPED · ALL WIRED · ALL READY TO G

8318

A.C. GILBERT
1884–1961
ERECTOR SET INVENTOR
S GAUGE PIONEER

BLT1-93

OPPOSITE TOP: By 1963 and 1964, A.C. Gilbert was backing away from the slow-selling S gauge toy train lines and moving toward more general toy products. "Hot Wheels" plastic car racing sets were big sellers with kids. Under the leadership of the Wrather Corporation, A.C. Gilbert offered this James Bond 007 road-race set. Licensing that name was not cheap, and the set failed to ignite big sales numbers.

OPPOSITE BOTTOM: A good idea that came too late, the All Aboard train system allowed kids to create a railroad layout from prefabricated, interlocking panels. The Pike Master track, which looked good but was not a good performer, and the cheesy train sets offered with the panel kits helped undermine the concept. The All Aboard train sets became known in the toy industry as one of the truly great flops of all time.

LEFT: A boxcar commemorating A.C. Gilbert and his Erector Set was shipped out by Lionel American Flyer in January 1993.

AMERICAN

FLYER

THE NAME CARRIES ON

eras. The wind-up and electric locos, with their little passenger cars, filled a need for fun toys in an awakening America before and after the Great War. The heady days of three-rail, O gauge electrics and steam trains, and big Wide gauge superstars of the late 1920s and '30s are part of legend now. But even they live on in reproductions from Lionel and Mike's Train House (MTH), so today's kids and adults with fond memories can see them in action at toy train shows.

It was A.C. Gilbert's era that was the most spectacular, though. With a vision of scale-model trains running on realistic two-rail track, he committed his company to giving kids the kind of trains he thought they really wanted. The man himself was an energetic entrepreneur who had made his mark long before he discovered toy trains. Nearly everything he touched was successful. And even in Gilbert's one failure, the company he built up left behind an incredible legacy that continues today—the joyous legacy of American Flyer trains.

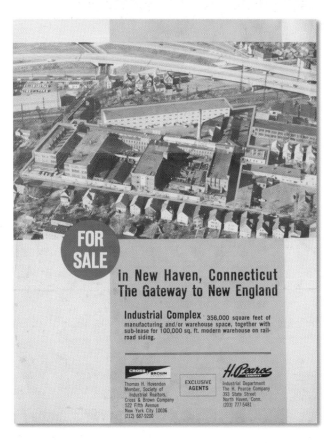

RESOURCES

OFFICIALLY SPONSORED
Even today you can still find American Flyer rolling stock on the Lionel website (www.lionel.com). True, only six cars are offered, but for the Flyer fan who is running the wheels off an aging consist, this is better than nothing.

CLUBS
To contact other American Flyer collectors, two organizations are always looking for new members:

The Train Collectors Association
The Train Collectors Association publishes two newsletters that often feature American Flyer articles: *The Train Collectors Quarterly* and *National Headquarters News*.
P.O. Box 248
300 Paradise Lane
Strasburg, Pennsylvania 17579
www.traincollectors.org

The Toy Train Operating Society (TTOS)
In California, the Toy Train Operating Society publishes the *Bulletin* and the *Order Board*.
25 West Walnut Street, Suite 308
Pasadena, California 91103
www.ttos.org

MAGAZINES
Classic Toy Trains
Kalmbach's magazine offers up numerous articles on American Flyer history and tidbits about locomotives and rolling stock.
21027 Crossroads Circle
P.O. Box 1612
Waukesha, Wisconsin 53187
www.trains.com

S-Gaugian
This a primary source for American Flyer information and should not be overlooked.
Heimburger House Publishing Company
7236 West Madison Street
Forest Park, Illinois 60130
www.heimburgerhouse.com/s.htm

BIBLIOGRAPHY

A.C. Gilbert Company Annual Reports, 1934–1936, 1951, 1955, and 1961. Courtesy of Andy Jugle.

Chaplin, Simon. Edited Steven H. Kimball. *Greenberg's Guide to American Flyer O Gauge*. Sykesville, Maryland: Greenberg Publishing Company, 1987.

Coleman Brown, Kirby. Interview by authors. Blowing Rock, North Carolina. 14 March 2002.

Coleman, Randolf. Interview by Bruce D. Manson in "Life with Father: The Toy Train Manufacturer," *The Train Collectors Quarterly*, October 1991.

Garrigues, Dave and Peter Jugle. "Electronic Propulsion Locomotives." In *A.C. Gilbert's Heritage*, edited by Don Heimburger. River Forest, Illinois: Heimburger House Publishing Company, 1983.

Gilbert, A.C. with Marshall McClintock. *The Man Who Lives in Paradise*. River Forest, Illinois: Heimburger House Publishing Company, 1990. Originally published in 1954 by Henry Holt & Co.

Hafner, John C. Interview by Peter Jugle. Tape recording. From the collection of Andy Jugle. N.d.

Hafner, Robert. Interview by Chris Rohlfing in *The Train Collectors Quarterly*, 16 July 1984.

Hollander, Ron. *All Aboard*. New York: Workman Publishing, 1981.

Kimball, Steven H. *Greenberg's Guide to American Flyer O Gauge*. Sykesville, Maryland: Greenberg Publishing Company, 1987.

Lazarus, Hilly. "The Colemans and American Flyer." Part 1 and 2. *Toy Train Operating Society Bulletin*, Vol. 16, No. 11, July 1981.

Lopes, George C. *American Flyer 1907–1940, Guide to O Gauge*. Self-published, 1997.

McLaren, Jack. "American Flyer Wide Gauge, 1926." *The Collector,* date unknown.

Nelson, Paul C. "A.C. Gilbert's Famous American Flyer Trains." In *A.C. Gilbert's Heritage,* edited by Don Heimburger. River Forest, Illinois: Heimburger House Publishing Company, 1983.

Overton, Richard C. *Burlington Route*. New York: Alfred A. Knopf, 1965.

Patterson, James C. *Greenberg's Guide to American Flyer S-Gauge*. Sykesville, Maryland: Greenberg Publishing Company, 1984.

Romer, Maury. Interview by Peter Jugle. "Looking at Gilbert Now." In *A.C. Gilbert's Heritage*, edited by Don Heimburger. River Forest, Illinois: Heimburger House Publishing Company, 1983.

Romer, Maury. Audiotaped by Dr. Ed Bernard. "Memories From My 40 Years at American Flyer: The Chicago Years." Part 1 and 3. *The Collector*, n.d.

———. "Memories From My 40 Years at American Flyer: The Chicago Years." Part 2. *The Collector*, Vol. 16, no. 3: Fall issue.

———."Memories From My 40 Years at American Flyer: The Gilbert Years—Conclusion." *The Collector*, n.d.

Romer, Maury and Bruce D. Manson Jr. "The Gilbert Hall of Science." *Train Collectors Quarterly*, n.d.

Schumacher, G.F. "Tooling for Toys." *Tool Engineering in Action*, December 1952.

Souter, Gerry and Janet. *The American Toy Train*. Minneapolis: MBI Publishing, 1999.

———. *Lionel, America's Favorite Toy Trains*. Minneapolis: MBI Publishing, 2000.

Tufts, Robert L. "American Flyer Tender Smoke Engines." In *A.C. Gilbert's Heritage,* edited by Don Heimburger. River Forest, Illinois: Heimburger House Publishing Company, 1983.

Walthers, Bill. *Walthers Craft Train News*, 15 April 1985.

INDEX

With the 1920s came American Flyer's "The Toy For The Boy" marketing slogan, and this 1922 catalog cover shows a smiling lad clutching his Flyer product. Note how prominently Flyer announces that its products were "Made in America," which was of importance especially in the days following World War I. The wings appearing beneath the American Flyer script give the boy a birdlike quality.

AMERICAN

FLYER

INDEX

A gleeful lad is at the throttle as the 4694 steamer and the President's Special roar past on their Wide gauge tracks on this 1930 American Flyer catalog. This is one of the last fanciful catalog covers as the later catalogs focused on prototype realism.

American Flyer Trains

Typical American Design···Years Ahead in New Features

One can almost hear the lonesome whistle of this passenger train hurtling down a stretch of Pennsylvania Railroad track at sunset. The last of the Wide gauge shelf inventory was being offered in this 1934 American Flyer catalog, but unbeknownst to fans, Flyer designers were hard at work with surprises for 1935.

GILBERT TOYS *American Flyer Trains* 1951

ERECTOR · CHEMISTRY · ATOMIC ENERGY · MAGIC · MICROSCOPE · TOOLS · PUZZLES

In 1951 Gilbert Toys, including Erector sets and magic kits, shared catalog cover space with American Flyer trains to pump up sales across the board. Because of the Korean War, Gilbert factories were busy with low-profit war work, so every toy had to pull its weight to keep sales numbers up.

In 1954, American Flyer was on a roll with their products. This catalog shows the GP-7 diesel, both as a single unit and as a double-header towing a dummy locomotive. The GP-7 in S gauge is one of Flyer's best-looking engines.

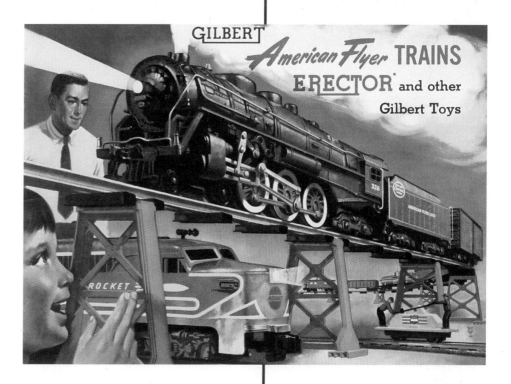

The catalog for 1958 was produced in full color. This was also the year that American Flyer's variety of offerings, colorful items, and customer appeal reached its peak. All the stops had been pulled out but, around the edges, reduction in quality was apparent. Motors were simplified and could be removed with a single screw. Double-unit passenger diesels became single-unit engines. And that year, the "World's Longest Train" was created with a figure-eight track setup. Headed by a hapless Atlantic, this train became the "Near Hit But Miss" set as the engine narrowly missed whacking the rear of the caboose at the track crossover.

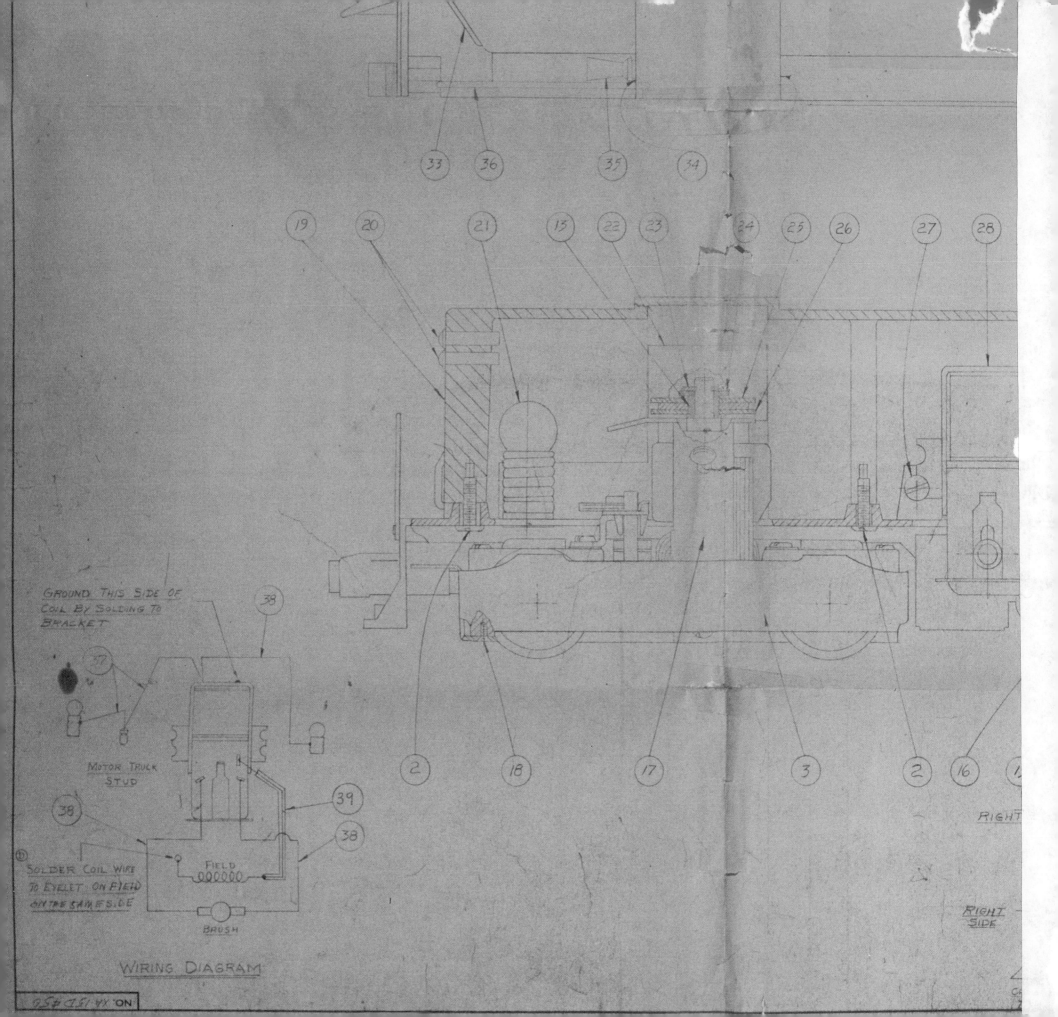

GROUND THIS SIDE OF
COIL BY SOLDING TO
BRACKET

MOTOR TRUCK
STUD

SOLDER COIL WIRE
TO EYELET ON FIELD
ON THE SAME SIDE

FIELD

BRUSH

WIRING DIAGRAM

RIGHT
SIDE

RIGHT

NO. XA 15(D 456